D1235301

CRAZY STORIES

FOR CURIOUS MINDS

Crazy Stories for Curious Minds

Strange and Unexplained Facts about History, Science, Mysteries, Pop Culture and Much More

Henry Bennett

GET TWO BONUS BOOKS FOR FREE!

To help you along your investing in knowledge journey, we've provided a free and exclusive copy of the short book, *Amazing Quick-Fire Facts,* and a bonus copy of book, *The Big Book of Fun Riddles & Jokes.*

We highly recommend you sign up now to get the most out of these books. You can do that by visiting https://www.subscribepage.com/henrybennett to receive your FREE copies!

To leave an Amazon review please visit
https://www.amazon.com/ryp or scan the QR code
below...

Table of Contents

Introduction

History is filled with strange, unusual, and sometimes downright weird stories. This collection of such stories will explore weird phenomena from all around our world and throughout time. Sometimes, the things that we think to be just myths are actually true facts and occurrences that cannot be explained!

Within the pages of this book, you will be introduced to such wild-but-true stories as that one time it rained eels in Alabama, or about the Turritopsis Dohrnii—a type of jellyfish that might just be immortal. You will find out about Hiroo Onoda—the very last Japanese soldier to stop fighting during World War II... 29 years after the war had ended.

Of course, if you are interested in some more mysterious things, we have you covered as well. Consider the "Babushka Lady," who might hold the key to the real murderer of President John F. Kennedy. You will also find other head-scratching mysteries inside of this book—and who knows! Maybe they will spur you on to find the truth, once and for all.

Did you know that President Abraham Lincoln's remains were almost stolen on one chilly, November night? Or that there is a river in Colombia that runs the colors of the rainbow? What about the great Tulip Bubble Burst in Holland?

If history and mysteries aren't exactly your thing, we also have grim stories of the supernatural and urban legends that will keep you up at night. Was that cry in the dark an Irish Banshee? How about the urban legend perpetuated in South Korea about your electric fan killing you in the middle of the night?

There are even stories of adventure and treasure included here. That includes the infamous Oak Island money pit—a pit so vast that the treasure within might be worth more money than you can imagine. There is also the story of Psyche 16—an asteroid that, if mined, could make every single person in the world a billionaire.

From Genghis Khan's thoughts on religion to the strange, colorful coffins of Ghana, this book will delight, amaze, and inform you. You will soon learn about the world's smallest police station, the correlation between a modern chicken and a fearsome Tyrannosaurus Rex, and much, much more!

These wild facts, histories, legends, and more can be found within the pages of this book. Strap in, get ready, and discover some of the most interesting, extraordinary, and peculiar facts from around the world and throughout time!

So, what are you waiting for?

Chapter 1:

The Purgatory of the Volkswagen Car

When one thinks of a graveyard, one might start to think of a place of mourning. This is where we bury our dearly beloved, after all; those that have passed on into whatever comes next.

We think of bones, coffins, and caskets, of old horror films. Maybe we think of peace and quiet, or a place to reflect. Whatever the case, we generally think of graveyards and cemeteries as places for the deceased. For *humans*.

However, scattered around the United States lay the remains of thousands upon thousands of Volkswagen vehicles. All of them are dead and decaying, left there seemingly to rot and rust. Why are they there? Why have those vehicles been left for dead, stuck in a sort of car purgatory?

Back in 2015, a whistleblower by the name of Hemanth Kappanna, along with a group of engineering students, revealed that the vehicle manufacturing company, Volkswagen, had been less than truthful about the extent of the emissions of their diesel vehicles. (Ewing, 2019) As part of the settlement that came out of this,

Volkswagen had to buy back around 350,000 of its diesel-fueled vehicles.

Of course, the next problem that Volkswagen found itself saddled with was where to put all of those 350,000 vehicles until they could recycle them. The short answer: America. The longer answer: in a plethora of car graveyards all over the country.

According to an NPR article published in 2018, there are 37 Volkswagen graveyard sites all across America (Wamsley, 2018). Each of these sites is massive—much, much larger than your typical parking lot. In the Detroit suburbs, for example, Volkswagen is using an old football stadium that was shut down years ago to house these vehicles. In the Californian desert, near Victorville, there is a massive stretch of land dedicated to being a vehicle graveyard.

These graveyards are rows upon rows of diesel-fueled vehicles. They are trapped there, in a sort of car purgatory, until Volkswagen decides what to do with them. It should be noted that Volkswagen has already destroyed and recycled some of these vehicles, with others being sold for scrap or parts—with most of those being sold to private buyers. The rest of them, however, simply sit and wait.

While Volkswagen does perform maintenance on the remaining cars within the graveyards—hoping to one day be able to sell them off again—for the moment, these vehicles are taking up a lot of space across the USA. Some are in old airports, some in the desert. Some are even taking up space in old factory buildings. There might come a day when their tires meet the road again, but for now, the future is looking rather bleak for these vehicles trapped in Volkswagen purgatory.

Chapter 2:

This Hole Came From Space!

In Arizona lies a massive crater. It is believed to have been formed roughly 50,000 years ago when a meteor struck the Earth (David, 2022). What's more, it is a training ground for astronauts today—as well as back in the 1960s.

The modern crew of the Artemis uses the crater in order to train for what it might be like on the moon. Scientists and members of NASA liken the crater to the surface of the moon. The terrain is similar enough for the crew members to perform basic training at the site.

Likewise, back in the 1960s, the crew of the Apollo missions trained in Meteor Crater.

Imagine standing in the center of a crater formed thousands of years ago by a fallen meteorite. It is vast and craggy, seemingly otherworldly. Yet it is right here, on Earth, in the state of Arizona. This one crater offers us a glimpse into what the moon's surface is like—pockmarked by craters—which is why it is so important and special for NASA's astronauts to train in and around it. What's more, it is considered to be the best-preserved meteorite crater on all of planet Earth. That makes it even more valuable.

When the crater was first explored back in 1891, it wasn't the idea of space that drew people to it. Rather, it was the massive amount of small diamonds that had been found in meteorites nearby. The meteorite that struck the Earth outside of Flagstaff, Arizona, came to be known as the Canyon Diablo meteorite.

In 1903, a mining engineer named Daniel Moreau Barringer saw the crater for the first time. He believed that he could unearth precious materials from the meteorite and make himself a very wealthy man. Because of this, Meteor Crater is sometimes known as the Barringer Crater. Barringer spent the rest of his life trying to learn more about the crater while also attempting to find those precious materials.

Unfortunately for Barringer, it would seem that most of the meteorite had been destroyed upon impact. Luckily for NASA, the crater is still in amazing condition, making it the best place on Earth—literally—for them to train those astronauts heading into space.

Luckily for us as well, there are tours of the crater. If you want to see what an astronaut would see when on the surface of the moon, it wouldn't hurt to check out Meteor Crater in Arizona.

Chapter 3:

The Hair-Raising Tale of the Fouke Monster

The year was 1971. Elizabeth Ford of Fouke, Arkansas, was curled up on the couch in her living room. Her husband, Bobby, and his brother, Don, were visiting elsewhere in the home. Everything was quiet and cozy; just a normal May evening.

Then, without warning, Elizabeth awoke when a hairy arm broke through the living room window. The creature on the other side was reaching for her, trying to steal her away—or worse, kill her outright. Elizabeth screamed, alerting Bobby and Don. The two men rushed in immediately, and then outside to chase away the beast.

During the hullabaloo, the creature managed to attack Bobby. It left minor scratches on him, but otherwise, the man was unharmed. Bobby and Don allegedly shot the creature, but there was so sign of blood or hair left behind.

Later, according to Bobby, he told police that he had seen an odd creature at the edge of his property prior.

He and his brother assumed it was a bear, and scared the thing off with a few gunshots.

Fouke, Arkansas, had just been visited by a monster.

This creature, looking similar to a Big Foot, soon became known around the country. Soon, it gained the nicknames "the Swamp Stalker" and "the Boggy Creek Monster." This is because of the landscape nearby Fouke—lots of bogs, swamps, and ponds. Plenty of space for a monster to hide.

The Fords's story became so popular that, one year after their monster encounter, a movie about the creature was released. It was called *The Legend of Boggy Creek* and ended up grossing over 25 million dollars (Monstro Productions, 2011).

The Legend of Boggy Creek was followed by *Return to Boggy Creek* in 1977, and later on in the 80s, *Boggy Creek II*.

Since the initial sighting of the creature, countless others have claimed to have witnessed the beast. Sightings of the monster have continued right up to modern day, including some in 2021. According to police reports, people have witnessed a large, orangutan-like creature at crossroads, or hikers have witnessed a similar creature along the side of forests (Monstro Productions, 2011).

In more recent years, Fouke has become the home of an annual festival celebrating the monster that made the area famous. The festival brings in cryptid hunters from around the globe, as well as just general fans of Big Foot and other such creatures. There are guided tours, food, games, and talks from Big Foot researchers and historians.

Chapter 4:

Why Was London Bridge Falling Down?

London Bridge is falling down,

Falling down,

Falling down.

London Bridge is falling down,

My fair lady.

(Blackwood, 2021)

These are the lyrics to a children's nursery rhyme, sung all around the world. Yet, how much do we actually know about the lyrics? What exactly does this little song mean—and how are the lyrics actually much darker than they seem?

Although similar rhymes had existed prior, in 1744, *Tommy Thumb's Pretty Song Book* was published (Blackwood, 2021). In this little songbook, the first official version of what became the London Bridge song we know now appeared.

London Bridge

Is Broken down,

Dance over my Lady Lee.

London Bridge,

Is Broken down,

With a gay Lady.

(Blackwood, 2021)

This version eventually evolved into the version we know now—but this does not explain why the lyrics are so odd, nor why they were changed. Throughout the years, historians have argued back and forth over what the lyrics actually mean.

Currently, historians almost all agree that the song is about a Viking attack in 1014 when the bridge was pulled down (Blackwood, 2021). That was not always the case; however, throughout the years, there have been many different ideas and thoughts on what the little nursery rhyme is about.

For example, the London Bridge was damaged throughout the years, most notably in 1666 during the great fires that swept through London (Blackwood, 2021). One author, Alice Bertha Gomme, suggests that the bridge was actually the site of human sacrifice, pointing to the lyric "take a key and lock her up" as proof of immurement, or the act of sealing a living person into a tomb or room without air, water, or food (Blackwood, 2021).

As for the London Bridge itself, the original London Bridge was torn down and replaced with a granite one. This was because it was too costly to repair (Blackwood, 2021). The replacement London Bridge was sold in 1962 by the British Government for 2.46 million dollars, plus the cost of shipping, to one Robert McCulloch (Londonist, 2013). It was painstakingly taken down, piece by piece, shipped to America, and rebuilt in Arizona—where it still stands today (Londonist, 2013).

Chapter 5:

The Enigma of Satoshi Nakamoto

Bitcoin. It has become a household name over the course of just a few years. It is a cryptocurrency that has recently gained popularity. With that in mind, one would think that the creator of such an innovation would be everywhere as well. Everyone would know their name, and who they are. There would be paparazzi following them everywhere.

This is where Satoshi Nakamoto should be. He should be a billionaire, rolling around in massive piles of money like a cartoon character. The acclaimed creator of Bitcoin—surely everyone knows his face?

All that is known about Satoshi Nakamoto is that he is not a real person.

For years, many have come forward to claim that they are Nakamoto. Time and time again, they have been debunked. Most recently, Craig Wright, who wrote a paper about Bitcoin in 2008, claimed to be the true creator behind Bitcoin (Milmo, 2022). He has been in and out of court over the possible ownership of Bitcoin.

Dr. Wright was originally brought to court by the estate of David Kleiman, who had been a former partner and colleague (Hayes, 2019). Kleiman's estate claimed that both men created Bitcoin together and that Dr. Wright owed the estate at least half of the wealth brought in via the Cryptocurrency.

Although the Kleiman estate was not awarded one-half of the overall wealth of Bitcoin, the court did award them roughly 100 million dollars—suggesting that the two had worked on the project together in some capacity (Hayes, 2019). The truth as to whether Dr. Wright and Kleiman created Bitcoin together is still a bit of a mystery; if Dr. Wright has the billions of dollars brought in by the Cryptocurrency, he is not telling anyone about it.

Another possible candidate is Dorian Nakamoto. He is a retired engineer living in California and was named as the creator of Bitcoin in 2014 by Newsweek reporter Leah McGrath Goodman (Hayes, 2019). Dorian Nakamoto denied any involvement with the creation of Cryptocurrency.

Whoever Satoshi Nakamoto is, they certainly aren't coming forward currently. This is one story that might remain a mystery for some time yet.

Chapter 6:

It's Raining Eels!

Coalburg, Alabama, is a small little hamlet where very little ever happens. It's a peaceful place, even though it's roughly eight miles from the city of Birmingham (spoonbillhank, 2019). Calm, quiet. Relaxing, really.

Except in May of 1892, when a massive rain cloud blotted out the sky. "Oh, just rain!" the townsfolk surely thought as they hurried inside of their homes. No need to get wet, after all. Yet, after the rain had started to fall, the people of Coalburg started to notice that the rain sounded strange.

One by one, everyone started to look outside. There, squirming in piles on the ground, were hundreds upon hundreds of live eels.

Some were up to a foot in length, while others were only an inch or two (spoonbillhank, 2019). They appeared to be young eels. That didn't matter much, of course—the people of Coalburg were mystified as to how and why it rained eels. What's more, the stench of the creatures after they passed on was atrocious, making it almost impossible to live in the town. Thankfully, nearby farmers took it upon themselves to collect the eels and use their bodies for fertilizer (spoonbillhank, 2019).

"Fish Rain" is an odd phenomenon that does occur from time to time. Scientists believe that waterspouts form over water, usually a lake or stream, and sort of suck up the fish into it. This waterspout then moves away from the water, up to a few miles, and turns to rain. When it rains, it pours, and in this case, it pours eels.

There have been recent "fish rains" as well. For example, in 2021, fish rained from the heavens in Texarkana, Texas. There have been instances of frogs and toads falling from the sky, as well as birds on the occasions when a small tornado formed near a flock. In some areas, it has rained snakes, bats, rats, mice, and other such small creatures (Korpar, 2021).

This brings a new sort of understanding to the term "It's raining cats and dogs!" Though, perhaps the saying should be changed to, "It's raining eels and fish!" Whatever the case, just be sure to bring your umbrella!

Chapter 7:

Ho Ho Ho—Away we Go!

Santa Claus. All across the world, people know who Santa Claus is. Children wait for his arrival every year, excited to receive gifts and candy on Christmas morning. Surely his job keeps him busy all of the time, whether it be preparing for Christmas or actually delivering the presents.

You might be surprised to learn, however, that Santa Claus has an official pilot's license! It would make sense; he flies everywhere, after all. Does that mean that his sleigh and reindeer are classified as an aircraft?

In 1927, Santa Claus was awarded an official pilot's license straight from the assistant secretary of commerce for aeronautics, William P. MacCracken (TAYLOR, 2020). A photograph was taken of the momentous occasion, and can now be found in the Library of Congress.

Today, many websites offer Santa Claus driver's licenses. These are used to make children believe that Santa had dropped his ID, giving a bit of magic to their Christmas mornings. While these fake IDs might be funny and charming, they are not replicas of the real ID that Santa Claus received in 1927.

So the next Christmas Eve, when your kids are tucked away for the night in their beds, rest assured that Old Saint Nicholas will arrive at your home soon, laden down with presents and stockings. Have some peace of mind—he's flying legally!

Chapter 8:

The Da Vinci Code?

When you think of great works of art, a few names might pop into your head. Michelangelo. Picasso. Van Gogh. One such name is Leonardo da Vinci—the creator of the masterpiece, the Mona Lisa. Yet da Vinci was much more than an artist. He was also an inventor, a teacher, and a musician (Dyslexia the Gift, 2016).

What do we really know about Leonardo da Vinci, however? We know that he was, for example, left-handed—which, for the time period, was seen as being rather unusual. We also know that he was probably dyslexic.

Da Vinci had the tendency to write messages by using mirrors. This allowed him to write backward. According to some researchers, this is something that many dyslexic, left-handed adults do in order to write in a more natural way (Dyslexia the Gift, 2016).

What's more, many historians believe that da Vinci might have had ADHD. This is because he often started many projects but rarely finished them, and he had horrible spelling abilities and handwriting (Dyslexia the Gift, 2016). Considering how beautiful and meticulous his art is, you can probably see why some people found this unusual during his lifetime.

There are plenty of mysteries surrounding the famous painter. Whether he was dyslexic; whether he had ADHD; or otherwise... The mysteries that surround da Vinci have both troubled and fascinated people throughout the centuries and across the globe.

Perhaps the most mysterious of his creations is the Mona Lisa. The Mona Lisa is perhaps one of the most recognizable pieces of art in the world—yet no one truly knows who the Mona Lisa is. Is she the portrait of a lady? A common peasant made to look lovely? Or, perhaps most shocking of all, is she a portrait of da Vinci himself, changed to make himself look like a beautiful woman?

According to a book written by scholar Lillian Schwartz, da Vinci's self-portrait matches perfectly with the facial structure of the Mona Lisa (Italy Magazine, 2007). Computer studies and scans of both pieces of art show that the bone structure of da Vinci's face, along with the shape of his nose, line up perfectly with the structure of the Mona Lisa's face—and that her smile is similar to how da Vinci's lips look when relaxed (Italy Magazine, 2007).

Why would da Vinci hide away behind the face of a beautiful woman? Some believe it was a prank da Vinci pulled in order to confuse his clients and commissioners. If it was a prank, it is certainly one that still holds up today.

For now, we must simply be content with the art and inventions da Vinci introduced us to. The man himself might just remain a mystery for the rest of time.

Chapter 9:

This Means (Whisky) War!

Hans Island is a small, rocky, inhabitable island located between Denmark and Canada. For years prior to Western colonization, it was used by the Inuit people as a hunting ground for polar bears (BLAKEMORE, 2022).

In the 1970s, when Canada and Denmark were redrawing their borders and territories, the two nations happened upon the little, unassuming island. Canada claimed to own it, while Denmark also claimed ownership. This turned into a bit of light-hearted scabbling, eventually escalating into the Whisky War.

A journalist from Greenland visited Hans Island in 1983 to write a story about some of the scientific activities on the island. Canada was, at that point in time, studying the area as a part of a possible area to drill for oil. The article drew the attention of the Foreign Minister of Denmark, who quickly took a helicopter out to Hans Island. It is said that the Foreign Minister left behind a Danish flag and some Danish alcohol as a bit of a joke.

This simple joke kicked off what was to become known as the Whisky War (BLAKEMORE, 2022). Both Canadian and Danish officials, scientists, and workers left numerous flags and alcohol bottles on the island as if to christen it anew.

Though this battleless war raged for decades, it is now at an end. In June of 2022, Denmark and Canada finally came to an agreement. Hans Island was split, with Greenland getting the larger half of the island, and Canada getting the smaller half (BLAKEMORE, 2022).

"Perhaps man-made boundaries only matter so much... More important is cooperation between people," said Danish foreign minister Jeppe Kofod at a press conference (BLAKEMORE, 2022).

Now the Whisky War is simply a footnote in the history of the world—a rather silly one, truth be told. At least there was no bloodshed—only whisky.

Chapter 10:

Genghis Khan Was More Progressive Than You Might Think

The Mongolians were a people of spiritual beliefs. They were shamanistic, meaning that they believed in the spirits of everything around them, from animals to stones and trees (Salem Media, 2017). Their leader, Genghis Khan, was thirsty for the knowledge of other belief systems.

It has been said that Genghis not only loved to learn about spirituality and religion, but he also saw them as aspects of human nature. As such, he was tolerant of every religion he came across—no matter how different from his own.

As the Mongolian empire grew, this did not change. No matter who they conquered, Genghis made sure that the religious bodies of each nation were spared taxation and allowed to continue to worship and preach (Salem Media, 2017). Even his sons, who had grown up with the same spiritual beliefs as their father, saw past differing religions. The women they married were from other religions, including Nestorian Christian women (Salem Media, 2017).

It was not just his sons that grew close with people from religions different from their own. Genghis Khan himself was known to make Muslims, Christians, and Buddhists into his personal advisors. He valued the opinions of all people, no matter what god they might worship.

Even the capital city of the Mongolian empire was a place of religious freedom and celebration. When it was founded, the city of Karakorum held no one religion over any other. Because of this, everyone was allowed to build places of worship without the fear of prejudice.

What's more, Genghis Khan believed in the freedom of speech. Though many aspects of history remember the Mongolians as barbaric, murderous people, they were actually very forward-thinking and civilized. Genghis Khan introduced many law practices that we still adhere to today. Without him, perhaps history would have been far different; maybe the seeds he sowed back then will finally flourish into a beautiful garden of all different beliefs and livelihoods today.

Maybe we should all be a little bit more like Genghis Khan.

Chapter 11:

Gunpowder Plot

In England, when the Queen visits Parliament, the cellars of the Palace of Westminster are searched and inspected *for explosives*. You might find this odd if you have never heard of Guy Fawkes.

Guy Fawkes was born in York in the year 1570. Both of his parents were loyal members of the Church of England (Loxton, 2019). When he was 21 years old, Fawkes joined the Catholic Spanish Army, having converted to Catholicism earlier in his life.

In the year 1604, Fawkes joined up with a group of other Catholics. This group was hellbent on ending the life of the then-current King—one King James. The reason they were itching to get him off of the throne was that he was a Protestant. There was a lot of civil unrest between the different branches of Christianity and Catholicism at the time, with people absolutely hating each other for being of different faiths.

The group of Catholics that Fawkes swiftly became friends with hatched a plot against the King. They wanted to do away with him in the hopes of getting his daughter, Princess Elizabeth, on the throne instead.

In order to carry out the assassination, the group decided to blow up the Houses of Parliament, along with anyone who happened to be inside. Originally, they had planned on tunneling under the buildings in order to fill up an underground space with volatile gunpowder.

As luck would have it, Fawkes was able to disguise himself as a servant. He managed to rent out the basement of the House of Lords. This saved the group from breaking their backs in digging out tunnels under Parliament.

Thirty-six barrels of gunpowder later, the team was ready to blow everything sky-high.

Unfortunately for the conspirators, and especially for Guy Fawkes, someone caught wind of their plan. The basement was searched and the gunpowder was seized. Fawkes was swiftly captured and questioned. Immediately and seemingly without regret, he claimed full ownership of the gunpowder and of the plot to kill the King.

While many people believed that Fawkes was burned for his crimes, he was actually tortured and hanged. On January 31, 1606, Guy Fawkes was executed. Perhaps he got the last laugh, however, as he went out on his own terms. It is said that, after the noose was put around his neck, Fawkes jumped. This purposely snapped his neck, keeping him from having to endure any other means of torture the law wished to impose on him.

Because of Guy Fawkes's gunpowder plot, the cellars of Parliament are still checked every year to make sure that no one else gets the bright idea to blow up the Houses with barrels of gunpowder.

Chapter 12:

No Dogs Allowed; Bears are Fine

Lord Byron is well known in modern times for being a romantic poet and a scandalous aristocrat (Humphrys, 2022). What many people don't know is that he was also once the owner of a pet bear.

In 1805, Byron started attending Trinity College at Cambridge. He desperately wanted to have a dog with him on campus, but the rules stated that no dogs were allowed. Enraged by how strict and, in his mind, stupid the rules were, Lord Byron decided that he was going to have the last laugh.

Soon, Byron purchased a tamed bear, probably from a traveling circus, though historians are not entirely sure of that. He claimed that the college had to allow him to keep the bear, as there were no rules against such a creature—only against owning a dog on campus. Legally, he argued, he could keep the bear.

After a bit of legal back and forth, it was decided that Byron was in the right; he would be allowed to keep the bear. It stayed with him in his room. Byron even took the bear for walks around the campus. Apparently, he got a real kick out of the shocked expressions of those he passed by.

At one point, Byron claimed that the bear should be able to attend college like a proper student. He claimed that the bear was intelligent enough to attend classes and that the bear was not a pet, but rather, a great friend.

Over the course of his life, Lord Byron kept many odd and unusual pets. He had the occasional dog or cat, but most of the time, he had pets like monkeys, crocodiles, peacocks, badgers, and multiple birds of prey (Humphrys, 2022).

The pet that ended up meaning the most to Byron, however, turned out to be a dog named Boatswain. This dog was the apple of his eye. Byron loved him so much that, when Boatswain caught rabies, Byron nursed him himself, without care that the dog might bite him and infect him as well (Humphrys, 2022). After Boatswain's passing, Bryon had a monument erected for him and even wrote in his will that he was to be buried beside the dog.

Chapter 13:

Now You're Playing With Power

Nintendo—it's easily one of the most recognizable names in video gaming. From Super Mario Bros to The Legend of Zelda and Animal Crossing, Nintendo has time and time again released amazing games for their home console systems, as well as for their handheld systems. Their latest system, the Nintendo Switch, is by far and away one of the most popular video gaming consoles currently on the market.

Yet none of that would be possible without hanafuda—beautifully painted and highly detailed playing cards.

Nintendo's first storefront was not one that sold video games. Rather, back in September of 1889, Fusajiro Yamauchi opened the first Nintendo store as a place to sell his hand-made hanafuda cards. His lovingly made cards were very popular, leading to him needing to hire extra workers fairly early on.

For the next 70 years, Nintendo was known for creating these beautiful and elegant playing cards. Unfortunately, in the 1960s, the cards became popular for gambling and soon grew to be associated with Yakuza. Yakuza are the Japanese mafia. Most things associated with them, including tattoos and hanafuda, are now looked down upon in Japanese society.

Luckily for Nintendo, the company gained a new leader—Hiroshi Yamauchi. Yamauchi was the great-grandson of the original founder of the company. He decided to take the card company in a new direction and decided to switch the focus of Nintendo's products from hanafuda to toys and arcade games.

Then, in the 1970s, Nintendo discovered a growing niche—video games. The company decided to put its hat into the ring, ready to try something new. This single action would go on to change the course of history when it comes to home entertainment.

By the 1980s, Nintendo had shifted pretty much all of its focus into creating an at-home video game console—the Nintendo Entertainment System, as it is known in the US. In Japan, it was known as the Famicom. The company released games featuring the character that would go on to be the figurehead of the company—Mario.

Other games were soon released, including the smash hits The Legend of Zelda, Donkey Kong Jr., and Tetris.

Nintendo had evolved from playing cards to gaming cartridges, and now, there's no looking back.

Chapter 14:

All Hail the Pirate Queen

At the start of the 19th century, piracy was in its glory. Ships sailed all over the world, looting and plundering. Many people know the names of some of these pirates— Blackbeard, Henry Morgan, Bartholomew Roberts, and countless others. Yet none of them can hold a candle against the true Pirate Queen, one Ching Shih.

Ching Shih, sometimes known as Cheng I Sao, or Zheng Yi Sao, lived during the Qing Dynasty. She ended up marrying the famed pirate, Cheng I. Cheng I was feared all along the southern reaches of China, known for his ruthlessness and his mass of ships and crew.

When Cheng I and Ching Shih married in 1801, Ching Shih was 26 years old. She was highly interested in piracy, actually managing the men and ships right alongside her husband. This was part of the reason why Cheng I wanted to marry her—Ching Shih had a reputation for being a very ruthless businesswoman. During her time on the mainland, she gathered secrets and interesting information concerning important people. She then used the secrets she learned to blackmail anyone she thought she could exploit, thus making both a name for herself and a lot of money.

Cheng I passed away after being married for six years, leaving his legacy to his wife. Little is known as to how or why Cheng I died. Ching Shih took over all of her husband's 1,800 ships and over 80,000 crew members. What's more, she ruled them. Ching Shih took what she had been handed and built it up, becoming a true Queen of the Pirates.

Ching Shih's reign was merciless. She had a very strict set of rules that her crew had to follow. Many of these rules concerned marriage aboard her ship—her men were allowed to marry, but if they did so, they had to promise to be faithful to their wives, no matter what. There were female pirates aboard her ships as well, and they were to be treated with the same respect as her male pirates.

In 1810, the Chinese government had had enough of losing their men to the Pirate Queen's fleet. They offered her amnesty, allowing her to retire in peace and with all of the money she had gained. It was really only around three years that Ching Shih's fleet terrorized the waters south of China, but the impact of her terror will last forever.

After retiring, Ching Shih lived a quiet life. She lived to the age of 69, passing away in 1844. Little is known about what exactly she did to occupy her mind during her retirement, as she sort of disappeared from society at large for most of it.

Chapter 15:

The War Ended 29 Years Ago!

Hiroo Onoda finally stopped fighting 29 years after the end of World War II. The Japanese soldier refused to believe, for almost thirty years, that the war had ended. During that time period, he hid in the jungles of Lubang Island, in the Philippines.

Born in March of 1922, Onoda was a rambunctious child, always ready for a fight. He was defiant of his elders as well. Stubborn to a fault, Onoda grew up in the village of Kamekawa in Wakayama, Japan.

Onoda's family had a long history of warriors, dating back to the fearsome samurai. Even his father, a sergeant in the Japanese cavalry, was considered a hero for fighting in the second Sino—Japanese war (Gabe Paoletti, 2017).

As such, when Onoda turned 18, he enlisted in the Japanese military so as to follow in the footsteps of his ancestors. One year later, Japan would go to war with America, following the attack on Pearl Harbor. While he was in the army, Onoda trained as a special intelligence officer, specifically learning unusual and sometimes unheard-of methods of combat. One of these methods was training in guerilla warfare—something he would find very useful in the years to come.

In December of 1944, Onoda and a small group of soldiers were sent to the small island of Lubang. The hold that the Japanese military had on the Philippines was growing weak due to the Japanese army spreading itself too thin, along with American troops now entering the playing field.

Onoda had one task on Lubang Island: Keep the island under Japanese control for as long as possible. That was a task that he took to heart.

On February 28, 1945, Japanese forces on Lubang Island were defeated by incoming American soldiers. Onoda, along with a handful of other specially trained Japanese soldiers, took to the jungle in guerilla warfare, ready to pick off the Americans one-by-one if needed.

For the next 29 years, Onoda and the men under his command survived off of stolen foods like rice, as well as what they could scavenge in the jungle. Although Onoda noticed that the fighting slowed around 1945, he refused to believe that the Japanese military had lost. He continued to fight, taking out Philippine soldiers and anyone else he considered a threat to his one task.

Every time someone, like the police, attempted to tell Onoda that the war was over, he fought them before disappearing back into the jungle. Even leaflets dropped by the American army claiming that the war had ended had no effect—Onoda just brushed them off as propaganda being spread by the United States in order to weaken the Japanese army.

Over the course of the next 29 years, Onoda's men either abandoned him or were killed by police when the group went to raid nearby villages for food. Eventually, Onoda was left alone, by himself, in the jungle. Still, he fought on—and continued to until 1974. That was when Norio Suzuki, a Japanese nationalist, went to the island of Lubang to find Onoda himself.

For quite a few years, Onoda's story had reached outside of the small island in the Philippines, all the way back to Japan. There, he had become a sort of urban legend— one that Suzuki desperately wanted to seek out.

Suzuki ended up spending some time with the old soldier, trying to get him to return to Japan. Onoda refused, stating that he had to be relieved of his duty properly before he would step down from war. When Suzuki returned to Japan, he spread Onoda's story, resulting in the Japanese government tracking down Onoda's commanding officer—who had become a book dealer in the years since the war. Major Yoshimi

Taniguchi officially relieved Onoda of his duties on March 9th, 1974.

And thus, the soldier was finally able to return to his homeland of Japan. For Onoda, World War II was finally over.

Chapter 16:

The Loudest Sound in History

The loudest sound in history came from the Krakatau volcanic eruption in 1883. The sound was so loud, so Earth-shattering, that it was heard well over 3,000 miles away.

Krakatau is a small, volcanic island in Indonesia. It is uninhabited—but that did not stop the eruption from affecting humanity all across the world. The eruption caused infrasonic pressure waves to rip through the Earth's atmosphere. These pressure waves rounded the planet not once or twice, but four times. This, in turn, caused massive tsunamis as far away as South Africa. Well over 36,000 people were killed due to these massive waves.

Thanks to the then recently invented telegraph, people everywhere were able to find out about the destruction caused by the volcano. It is considered to be the first natural disaster that affected the entire world at once in recorded history.

Although the sound that was created by the infrasonic pressure waves is actually too low for humans to hear, it is also thought to be the loudest sound ever in human history. We, as humans, would not be able to hear the sound, but our bodies would be able to feel it.

It is believed that the sound actually lasted for five entire days, though at the time, there were no scientific instruments capable of recording the sound as a sound. There were, however, barometers, which started to record the sound via a sort of drawing and graphs. Scientists in the current day have attempted to recreate the sound on a smaller scale, though it is still a lot of guesswork as they are going off of notes and records instead of the sound itself.

According to some of these records, people actually thought that the explosion was the end of the world. That was how powerful the unheard sound was—it shook the Earth. In London, barometers were going haywire in an attempt to record the noise—but the sound was literally off of the charts.

Meanwhile, places closer to the eruption were recording and reporting that massive rocks were falling from the sky, taking out buildings and bridges. The air was so thick with ash that it was impossible to see the sky.

As of now, no sound has been able to rival the eruption of Krakatau.

Chapter 17:

Jack's Been Working on the Railroad

James Wide, better known as Jumper, once worked for the railway system in Cape Town, South Africa. He was an energetic man, having received his nickname from jumping from train to train as they entered and exited the train yard. Then, misfortune struck—in 1877, Jumper jumped at the wrong time. The end result was that both of his legs were severed at the kneecap.

Undeterred by his injuries, Jumper decided he wanted to continue working for the railway system. After he recovered and was equipped with two homemade wooden legs, Jumper started to work for Uitenhage Station. While he enjoyed his work, it was difficult at times since it was a job that required a lot of moving around.

One day, Jumper ran into Jack. Jack was skillfully leading a team of oxen through a busy marketplace and made quite an impression on Jumper. He decided that Jack just *had* to work with him—so he worked out a deal with Jack's owner.

Oh, about that—Jack was a baboon.

Over time, Jumper was able to train Jack to do a number of things around the train station, including pulling levers and retrieving keys for conductors. What's more, Jack was able to push Jumper around in a makeshift wheelchair, making Jumper's job a lot easier.

Jumper and Jack were able to sort of communicate through a series of hand signals and whistle blasts. Jack knew what every command meant, what every blow of the whistle was signaling. As he learned, he began to take things on for himself without being asked—like handing over keys to the correct person. Eventually, he was so good at his job that, with only a little supervision from Jumper, Jack was able to control the train signals on his own.

Rather quickly, Jack gathered a lot of notoriety. Not all fame is good; however, many worried passengers were calling for Jack and Jumper to both be fired. Many people did not see the man and monkey team as anything good; rather, they feared that they were going to get people killed.

A railway manager was dispatched quickly to the station, ready to fire both Jumper and Jack. Jumper, however, managed to convince the manager to give Jack a chance. The manager, expecting the monkey to be incapable, allowed the team to humor him. Soon enough, he was blown away by how efficient Jack truly was. So much so that he allowed Jumper to keep his job—and made Jack an official employee who was paid 20 cents per day, with the bonus of a bottle of beer at the end of every week (Serena, 2017).

Sadly, after nine years on the job, Jack passed away due to complications from tuberculosis. His skull, though, can still be found in a museum in Grahamstown, South Africa.

Chapter 18:

The King of Kings

Darius the Great was the king of the Achaemenid Empire in Persia from 522 to 486 B.C.E. (Hodsdon, 2021). During this period of time, the Persian Empire was in the golden years of its time period—and much of that is due to Darius the Great's efforts.

Darius was born in 550 B.C.E. to Hystaspes. Hystaspes was a general in the Achaemenidian army, as well as a member of the royal court. During his early life, Darius was a loyal member of the royal court and the royal army, serving as a spearman to the then-Prince, Cambyses. The two apparently had a very close bond during that time period, with Darius happily serving under him. It probably helped somewhat that the two were cousins as well as friends.

One day, while Cambyses and Darius were visiting Egypt, a revolt broke out. A man by the name of Gaumata had decided that he wanted to rule the Persian empire, along with a small group of followers. According to written accounts from Darius the Great himself, Gaumata had impersonated Prince Bardiya, Cambyses' younger brother. It is possible that Gaumata had assassinated the prince, taking his place in secret.

Quickly, Cambyses and Darius returned to Persia. On their way, however, Cambyses suffered an injury after being thrown from his horse. The wound festered and grew to be infected, later killing the prince before he could return home.

Carrying on in his place, Darius and a few other members of the royal court returned to Persia and took out the false prince. Once he was out of the way, and with Cambyses dead, the nobles had to figure out who the new king would be.

In order to figure out the new king, the nobles held a contest. Each of them would sit on top of their preferred horse, and whichever horse neighed at day's first light would be the horse of the new king. It is said that Darius cheated by tampering with his horse at just the right time, leading him to neigh just as the sun broke over the horizon. Thus, Darius was declared king.

Darius' rule did not pass by without some pushback, however. There were many attempts for other nobles to overthrow him and take the throne for themselves. King Darius crushed any and all attempts to overthrow him; however, traveling across the Persian empire to stamp out any revolts.

During his reign as king, Darius was actually very well known for expanding the size of his empire, as well as fixing the somewhat broken tax system that had come with the kingdom. He worked extremely hard at bettering the economy, not just for nobility, but for the common man as well. What's more, he declared that everyone should be tolerant of other religions around them and within their own society. He preached peace between the different religions.

After 36 years of ruling, King Darius finally passed away due to health complications. This was before he could take control of Greece; at the time of his death, the Persian Empire was attempting to seize control of the other country.

Chapter 19:

Hollywood, Hollywoodland

The Hollywood sign is, perhaps, one of the most recognizable landmarks in the United States. It has been seen in hundreds of films and television shows, and many people travel from all around the world just to see it for themselves.

This has not always been the case, however. The sign, originally, didn't even say "Hollywood" as we know it today. No, back then, the sign, with its blinking lights and bright white paint, used to read "Hollywoodland."

During the 1920s, California was an up-and-coming place to live. Spurred on by the lasting impact of the gold rush in the 19th century, California became the go-to place to live (Braudy, 2018). Then, in 1923, a real estate group that was backed by Harry Chandler—a well-known Los Angeles Times publisher—built the Hollywoodland sign as a way to announce a new housing development. That's right—the famous sign was originally nothing more than a marketing ploy to draw new homeowners into the area.

In the late 1940s, it was decided that the sign should be taken down. This was a large undertaking, as the hill that the sign sits on is extremely steep. Furthermore, the sign itself is much larger than it appears to be—and it's made of cut sheet metal adhered to telephone poles. When it was first built, it was really meant to be a one-time thing; a throw-away piece of advertising. Getting the entire sign down was going to be a difficult task.

However, before the sign could be torn down forever, the Hollywood Chamber of Commerce made a deal with Los Angeles; they would take over the sign's maintenance and care in exchange for the 'land' portion of the sign being removed.

From that point until well into the 1970s, though the sign had become a cultural landmark, the actual upkeep of it was rather rough. There were patchwork jobs here and there, and sometimes a new paint job, but it was generally ignored by the Hollywood Chamber of Commerce.

In 1978, the famous Hugh Hefner and Alice Cooper collected roughly $27,000 per letter in order to rebuild the sign from the ground up.

Now, the Hollywood sign stands as a testament to the cultural growth of the film industry. It is recognizable to people all around the world.

Chapter 20:

Alþingi

Alþingi, sometimes written as Althing or Althingi, is a part of Iceland. It was founded way back around 930. Its parliament is one of, if not the, oldest parliaments in the world.

In 930, Alþingi was formed so that those with seats of power—leaders and of the like—could decide on and argue for different laws and restrictions for the area. Any and all freemen in the area could attend, which meant that anyone save for slaves could show up to Alþingi to air their grievances. All around Alþingi's center, freemen would set up camps while the court was in session. This meeting area was called Thingvellir.

Thingvellir is now a historical site in the southwest of Iceland. Between the years 930 and 1798, Thingvellir was the meeting place of the Alþingi parliament. It is now a national park. Very few of the original buildings from the 930s remain, most of them just rubble at this point.

In medieval Scandinavia, the Althing, meaning *all freemen*, was the first body of people to exercise legislative power at such a wide scale, and specifically, at the national level (The Editors of Encyclopaedia Britannica, 2022).

Up until the mid-1200s, the freemen and their leaders would meet at Alþingi. However, in 1262, Iceland changed. It was now under the rule of the Norwegian King, meaning that the meeting of leaders and freemen came to a close. Everyone had to listen to the King, and no one else was allowed to give their opinion or champion for what they felt was right.

In the early 1800s, the Alþingi was demolished by the Danish Crown. However, in 1845, the Alþingi was reinstated in the capital city of Iceland, Reykjavík, and has remained there since.

Specifically, the parliament house stands in Austurvöllur square within Reykjavík's city. It was built in the early 1800s and has since been added to. It also contains the oldest public garden in Iceland.

Chapter 21:

The Sand Dunes of Japan

Japan is a beautiful country. It is widely known for its mountains and forests—but did you know it has an area of just sand and gloriously high dunes?

The Tottori Sand Dunes are the largest sand dunes in all of Japan (LaGrave, 2017). The dunes reach a height of about 165 feet. Coming in at only about a mile wide but nine miles long, these sand dunes are sort of Japan's secret desert. They are located in the Tottori prefecture, thus giving these golden hills of sand their name.

The area has become a major tourist attraction. There are areas to hike, but there are also camel rides and horse-drawn carriages to take you around if you don't feel like walking.

Although it is not very well known outside of Japan, for the Japanese people, the sand dunes are a national treasure. What's more, they have been featured in different poems and novels over the course of the last few decades, making them a must-see attraction. Some people even consider the area to be hauntingly romantic probably due to a poet who committed suicide with his lover shortly after visiting and writing about the dunes.

Many people consider the Tottori Sand Dunes Japan's desert. While it might look that way to the untrained eye, the dunes cannot be classified as a desert properly. This is because the climate is not arid, as it would be in a proper desert. Secondly, the area around the Tottori Sand Dunes is not sparse or barren. In fact, some people have reported being able to see the Sea of Japan from the top of the dunes. There is also a forest nearby, making the landscape more lush than barren.

While the sand dunes are a very popular place to visit, with well over 2 million tourists checking them out every year, the dunes themselves are starting to shrink. This is due to growing vegetation in the area and the changing of winds. For now, the sand dunes are a glorious thing to behold; before long, however, they will be just a memory, like sand slipping through an hourglass.

Chapter 22:

From Here to Timbuktu

Many people have heard the phrase "from here to Timbuktu." People may have heard of Timbuktu, but thought it was maybe a fictional or mythical place. The history of the actual Timbuktu, in Mali, is much more interesting than any old sayings, though.

Timbuktu was founded around the 5th century. It wasn't until the 15th and 16th centuries, however, that Timbuktu became the cultural and economical giant it is best known for (Bate, 2021). Trade routes passed through and by Timbuktu as things like salt and precious metals were hauled from one area to another.

Slowly but surely, Timbuktu became a sort of trade hub. People from all around came to buy and sell wares. It soon grew to be a popular spot for intellectuals within the Muslim religion as well. It even housed the University of Sankore, which helped to spread the Muslim religion during that time period.

Originally, Timbuktu was a part of the Mali Empire. Eventually, through the years, it became a part of the Songhai Empire. In the 16th century, the Songhay

Empire collapsed, and with it, so did Timbuktu's social-economical hold on the world.

Fast forward to today. While most of Timbuktu is lost to the ages, there are a few historical sites that still exist. This includes the holy site of the Dyingerey Ber Mosque. Visitors to the area can even tour the mosque.

The historical site of Timbuktu also includes a library of many religious texts, making it a place for scholars and religious peoples alike. This is, sadly, only a ghost of what it used to offer. There is also a historical graveyard for World War II soldiers who passed away there. Merchant ships and sailors were held in Timbuktu during the war.

More recently, the Flame of Peace was erected to honor the Tuareg rebellion.

Timbuktu is located in the Sahara desert. While you are able to visit it, it is highly recommended that you do so with a guide and that you have done plenty of research into the area's climate. Some historians at the site suggest not going, as it can be a very dangerous area of the world to explore.

Chapter 23:

Fish-Shaped Coffins

In Ghana, funerals are both a time of mourning and a time of celebration. There, it is believed that the afterlife starts right after death—and that those who passed on should have a celebration in order to introduce them to their afterlife.

Due to this, it is very common in Ghana to have an interesting coffin to guide you into the hereafter. This tradition is known as *abebuu adekai* (CNN, 2016). It all started in the 1950s when a tribal leader passed away in his carriage. The carriage was made to be in the shape of a cocoa pod. When the leader died, his retainers decided to simply bury him in the pod-shaped carriage—thus creating the idea of fun and interesting coffins.

The incident inspired a carpenter, one Seth Kane Kwei, to start a business centered around creating and carving interesting and thoughtful coffins. For example, the first coffin he created was for his own grandmother. This special coffin was shaped to look like an airplane—the woman had never managed to travel via a plane, though she had wanted to for her entire life. What better way to send her off into her afterlife than in her own, private plane?

After he had created a specialty coffin for his grandmother, other orders started to pour in. A fishing boat for a beloved fisherman. A piano for a musician, and so forth. Many of the apprentices who ended up working for Kane Kwei later left to start their own businesses, either in coffin making or for other studios.

Because these coffins are all handmade and crafted, there is a bit of a wait for them. One coffin by itself might take many weeks to produce. The coffins are generally made from lightweight woods, though there have been special orders that use more expensive and heavier materials. Most of the coffins are priced at around 1,000 dollars, though there have been instances of the price rocketing up to almost 8,000 dollars.

These coffins have become so popular that there are people outside of Ghana who order them. While shipping costs are astronomical, the different coffin studios are more than happy to export their goods. Some of the coffins have even been considered works of art, and have been shown off at museums as far away as London.

The coffin business in Ghana started with an airplane, lovingly made for a grandmother. Now, that same airplane model is extremely popular and is one of the studio's most requested coffin designs. Other designs include animals such as roosters and fish; cameras for those who loved photography; art supplies like pens or pencils for those who loved art; fishing boats; pianos and other musical instruments; and even things like machine guns.

If you are going to have one last party before you depart to the afterlife, why not make it fun? Why not go in style with a coffin shaped like something important in your life? It's certainly one way to make an exit from this life—and an entrance into the next.

Chapter 24:

The Death of a Great

Alexander the Great. The man. The myth. The legend. Most of the people in the world have heard of him. There are many great stories surrounding the man—but who was he, exactly? And, furthermore—how could someone as powerful and great as Alexander die?

According to historical records, he was "...born in 356 B.C.E. at Pella in Macedonia, the son of Philip II and Olympias (daughter of King Neoptolemus of Epirus)" (Walbank, 2018). In his teenage years, he was taught by Aristotle himself. While Alexander and Aristotle shared a lot of the same ideas, Alexander did not share the belief that non-Greeks should be treated as slaves.

Alexander proved himself to be a fearsome commander in the army, besting some of the worst enemies Greece had seen.

In 336, Alexander's father, Philip II, was assassinated. Alexander took over his father's seat without any sort of opposition. From there, he went on to conquer the Persian Empire, followed by the Asian Minor, the Mediterranean Coast, Egypt, and other parts of the world.

Then, after a short reign, Alexander the Great fell. After a party in June 323, Alexander fell ill. He died shortly thereafter—but why? Throughout the years, there have been many different theories as to how the great leader died, and why.

Despite the huge impact he had on the world, Alexander the Great was still relatively young when he passed away—he was only 33 years of age. Some people believe that he died due to alcohol poisoning, considering it was shortly after a very large party where he was recorded as having a lot of alcohol. Others, though, claim that he must have been poisoned by someone who wanted him dead.

Others theorize that he died of either typhoid fever or malaria. Both illnesses were running rampant in Babylon, which was where he passed away. According to the records taken from his time period, his symptoms seemed to closely fit either disease, with typhoid fever being the most likely.

No matter how he died, Alexander the Great led a life so intense and powerful that we still know about him today. He left a legacy in history that will never be forgotten.

Chapter 25:

Scream Queen

She arrives in the dead of night, knocking upon your door. Her hair is long and wispy, falling around her face, framing the hollow glow of her eyes. There is a shriek in the air, ripping through the peaceful darkness.

The Banshee has come for you. There is no escape.

The Banshee is perhaps one of the most fearsome creatures to come out of Irish folklore and legend. She is sometimes known as the Hag of the Mist or the Hag of the Black Head (Brent, 2021). More often than not, she is pictured as an old woman with long, white hair that floats around her gaunt face. Her eyes are usually either completely hollow or glowing unnaturally. The worst part about her, however, is her scream.

When you hear a Banshee scream, it's far too late for you. The ghostly hag screams when she can feel death nearby; if you hear her shriek, you are going to die soon. If not you, then one of your very close family members. The scream is said to be loud enough and powerful enough to shatter windows and break down doors.

The name "Banshee" is derived from Old Irish, meaning "a woman of the fairy mound" (Brent, 2021). The "mounds" here refer to the mounds made on fresh graves. These graves were said to be home to new spirits and ghosts.

Originally, the stories of the Banshee can be dated back to around the 1300s, and similar creatures have been recorded in Welsh and Scottish folklore. In the earliest stories of the Banshee, there were three different forms she would take. The first was the shape of a young woman. This young woman would sing a beautiful, haunting song in the hopes of drawing young men to their deaths. This is similar to the idea of a Siren or mermaid.

The second shape the Banshee might take is that of an adult woman. Not too young so that she could be called a maiden, but not yet old enough to be considered a crone. In this shape, the Banshee was known for singing as well.

The third shape is the one that is most well known—the old hag. This form searches for those near death. She will scream at them if they look at her; furthermore, she has been known to knock on doors late at night in an attempt to catch the soon-to-be-deceased.

It is said that no matter what form she takes when she comes for you, the Banshee will always be wearing old, tattered clothing, usually either white or gray in color. Her eyes will be bloodshot and red from sobbing and screaming so hard. What's more, it's said that her skin will be deathly pale.

The idea of the Banshee might have started with war, of all things. Soldiers would apparently hear moaning or screaming in the forest—probably some kind of animal—and would thus retreat out of fear. In doing so, they would be killed by their commanding officers for retreating, or they might run into a trap set up by their enemies. As this happened more and more, the other soldiers would start to tell stories of the terrifying Banshee—a harbinger of death.

Chapter 26:

Immortality, Jellyfish Style

What would you do to become immortal? Would you allow a vampire to bite you? Would you make a deal with a demon? Would you willingly become... a jellyfish?

The jellyfish species Turritopsis Dohrnii has the unique distinction of being the only immortal creature known to mankind. They were first discovered in the 1880s, floating around in the Mediterranean Sea (AMNH, 2015).

All jellyfish, believe it or not, start out their life as larvae. This is similar to how insects age; they have different life stages. When it finally grows into the jellyfish shape we know today, the Turritopsis Dohrnii is tiny—not even an inch wide. This kind of jellyfish has about 90 tentacles. The jellyfish itself is small and hard to see, as it has a transparent body for the most part.

What is most fascinating about the Turritopsis Dohrnii, however, is that when it is damaged in any way, or it is starving, its body will start to automatically regenerate. They do this by literally rewinding themselves back into their larval stage. This allows them to heal up whatever was wrong with them—and then they just progress through their life cycle again until something else happens to physically damage them. This process is called transdifferentiation and is extremely rare.

Scientists in the medical field have started to study the Turritopsis Dohrnii in hopes of being able to use the process of transdifferentiation in medicine and medical procedures. Specifically, scientists are hoping that this process can be used to help people who have lost certain cells due to illness and disease.

Aside from being immortal, the Turritopsis Dohrnii likes to travel. They have been known to hitch rides on the sides of ships as they pass through their waters, using this as a mode of transportation so that they can explore new areas.

There is still a lot to learn about these immortal jellyfish. Only time will tell as to how they will help the medical field. While it might be finite for us humans, time, after all, is all that the Turritopsis Dohrnii have.

Chapter 27:

Down Undah

In the 1980s, for some reason, American media was obsessed with Australia. "Down Undah" became a talking point for the average American, with the country being recognized in songs, books, and most importantly, films.

"Crocodile Dundee" was a popular film that came out in 1986. It was made on a 10 million dollar budget as an attempt at making an Australian film to be marketable overseas (Jensen, 2017). It starred actor Paul Hogan, playing the role of Michael Dundee, and was the story of an Australian bushman going into the big city for the first time.

What most people do not realize is that the character of Michael Dundee was based on a very real man.

That's right—the Crocodile Dundee was actually a man by the name of Rodney Ansell. Ansell loved the wilds of Australia. As early as the age of 15, he had moved into the northern area of the country, hunting down wild buffalo. He made a living by selling the meat.

In 1977, Ansell was on a fishing trip when his boat was capsized by an unknown animal. While in later interviews Ansell claimed it to be a whale, it was more likely a very large crocodile in the Victoria River (Jensen, 2017). Ansell quickly gathered up what few items he could. That left him with a few supplies and his two puppies—one of them with an injured leg. After passing out, he, his scant supplies, and the puppies were washed ashore on an island at the mouth of the Fitzmaurice River (Jensen, 2017). This island, for the next 56 days, would be Ansell's only home.

Ansell used his survival skills to find honey and fresh water, as well as hunt and fish. At night, he and his dogs slept in the trees to keep out of the reach of hungry crocodiles. He later claimed that he was sure he would never be rescued—he had told everyone before the fishing trip that he would be gone for a few months, so no one realized at that point that he was missing.

Then, one day, Ansell heard two Aborigines and their white companion nearby. He hailed them, and they managed to rescue him, taking him back to civilization.

Ansell's story soon spread like wildfire. He quickly became a media darling, and even wrote a book about his adventures. When the film Crocodile Dundee was being written, a lot of inspiration was taken from Ansell's book.

Unfortunately, Ansell did not receive any sort of compensation from the film. He later tried to capitalize on the movie by calling his tour business 'The Real Crocodile Dundee Adventure Tour," but Paramount Pictures, who had distributed the film, threatened him with a lawsuit (Jensen, 2017).

Ansell died in 1999 after an accident involving two police officers. He was buried on Aboriginal land.

Chapter 28:

Death by Fan

Many people fall asleep with their electric fans on. Some of these people do this with the window shut. However, in South Korea and parts of Japan, this simple act is one that strikes fear in the populace. Why? Because, according to an urban legend, falling asleep with an electric fan on and the window shut can kill you.

This myth has gained so much popularity that, in South Korea, most electric fans are built with a timer in them. After a certain period of time, they will automatically turn off—a sort of fail-safe, if you will. Even the owners of electronics shops are afraid of the myth—take Kim Yong Ho, for example. When interviewed, he claimed, "I would turn the timer on and make sure the winds were blowing very gently. I'd also make sure the fan head is rotating around the room" (SHAPIRO, 2015).

It seems that there are many reasons why South Koreans believe that a running fan in a closed room can kill a person. Some believe that the fan will blow too much cold air into the room, causing the temperature to plunge. Hypothermia, then, would be the cause of death in this instance. Still, others claim the opposite—that sitting in an enclosed room with a fan will make the temperature too high since the fan cannot cycle in any fresh air. This leads to people apparently dying due to high temperatures. Still, others believe that the fan will somehow suck up all of the oxygen in the room, leading to asphyxiation.

One scientist, Chun Rim, decided to run a few tests concerning the myth in 2008. Since he could not find anyone to volunteer to stay in a room with a fan, he decided to enlist the aid of his then 11-year-old daughter.

Chun Rim claims that he checked up on his daughter every few minutes to make sure that she was safe (SHAPIRO, 2015). He checked all of her vitals and recorded them. His daughter was fine, though perhaps a little tired at being woken up every so often. In the end, Chun Rim concluded that the urban legend of fan death is just that—an urban legend. He and his family are no longer afraid to leave their fans on at night when they sleep.

Despite these tests, the fear of dying by fans in South Korea is still thought of as being completely valid. While it is debatable if anyone has actually died from a fan in an enclosed room, the legend still lives on today.

Chapter 29:

Snoop Doggy Dogg

Calvin Cordozar Broadus Jr. was born on October 20, 1971, in Long Beach, California. When he was a child, he loved singing and playing the piano at his local church (Greer, 2022). Then, his life changed forever in grade school—Calvin discovered rap music.

As he grew up, Calvin ended up on the wrong side of the law. He joined a gang associated with the Crips, thus ending up in and out of jail for some time (Greer, 2022). Thankfully, during this time period, he started to record himself when he sang or rapped. These mixtapes eventually fell into the hands of none other than Dr. Dre, a famous musician and producer.

Calvin ended up working with Dr. Dre, taking on the stage name of Snoop Dogg, in 1992. His music, with help from his producer, launched his rapping career. The rest, as they say, is history. Yet one major question still remains—

—Why the name "Snoop Dogg?"

In a 2009 interview, Snoop Dogg explained that he received his stage name from the "Peanuts" character,

Snoopy. When he was a child, he explained, he loved watching the show as it aired on television. Snoopy soon became his favorite character. From there, he started to call himself Snoop Dogg in honor of the animated beagle.

He stated, "As a kid born in the [the 1970s], mom used to put on a TV show called Charlie Brown. And there was a character on there named Snoopy. And I used to love him to death... And my mama said I started to look like him so much 'cause I watched him all the time, and that's what they used to name me." (Greer, 2022)

Throughout his career, Snoop Dogg has attempted to change his stage name a few times—but in the end, "Snoop Lion" and "The Dogg Father" simply didn't stick the same way that Snoop Dogg does.

While those in the older generations remember Snoop Dogg for his music, many people these days know him from his cookbooks and his friendship with Martha Stewart.

Chapter 30:

The Spy Who Disappeared

Lionel Crabb is a name that not many are familiar with. He was a commander in the 1950s and was often sent on spying missions that involved underwater diving. It was during one of these missions in 1956 that something went horribly wrong—and it ended with Crabb's death.

Crabb was not exactly at the peak of health. He was 47 years old at the time of his death, possibly an alcoholic, and a chain-smoker (bob.hind1, 2019). Still, his death was one that the British government did not want to admit to. Because of that, they covered up his death and the mission he died on, cleaning things up as though Crabb never existed, to begin with.

Unfortunately for the government, the media caught wind of the cover-up, quickly exposing them in their attempts to wipe the slate clean of Commander Crabb. To combat this, the government swiftly set up an embargo on the disclosure of the facts having to do with the failed mission (bob.hind1, 2019). The ban was to last one hundred years; only then, after that much time had passed, would the truth be revealed.

No one really knows what happened to Crabb after he went under the water. There have been a few ideas, however, and even some people coming forward over the years to claim that they had something to do with the frogman's disappearance and assumed death.

One such man was Eduard Koltsov, a retired Russian sailor (SAINSBURY, 2021). In 2007, at the age of 74, Koltsov admitted to killing Crabb on that fateful day. he stated that he did so because Crabb had attached a bomb to the side of the ship Koltsov was stationed on—something that would have been highly illegal at the time. Many have dismissed Koltsov's claims, saying that he just wanted some sort of attention or fame.

Other theories claim that Crabb was taken hostage by Russian sailors. Considering that, at the time, the Cold War was really starting to ramp up, and considering that Crabb was a known spy, it is probable that the Soviet Union sailors thought that they could take Crabb and gather some kind of important intel from him.

Whatever the case, Crabb's death is still a mystery, even to this day. That, however, did not stop author Ian Fleming from basing the world's most famous spy on Crabb's exploits. That's right—Lionel Crabb was one of the major inspirations for 007—James Bond himself.

Chapter 31:

Heist at the Museum

It was the morning of March 18th, 1990. The Isabella Stewart Gardner Museum, seated in Boston, stood just as it had any other day. Inside were hundreds of priceless paintings and art pieces. Two policemen entered the building. No one seemed to pay them any mind; it was not unusual to see police officers out and about, after all. Perhaps they were just on a break. Perhaps they were guarding something within the museum or helping to transport a new piece into the museum's library of art.

Or, perhaps, they were getting ready to pull off one of the largest heists in history.

Those two police officers were actually art thieves. No one knows, even to this day, who they were or how they were able to steal thirteen pieces of art from the Isabella Stewart Gardner Museum. No one knows where those thirteen pieces of art are now. That's right—over thirty years later, the theft is still unsolved. Thirteen pieces of famous art—valued at around half of a billion dollars—are still missing.

Included in those lost artworks is Johannes Vermeer's *The Concert*. This piece, from the mid-1600s, is considered to be one of the rarest missing pieces of art (Schwartz, 2018). Very few of Vermeer's paintings exist currently, and historians cannot decide if three of the supposed 37 are forgeries or not. The painting in question is considered to be one of calm, despite the focus being on three musicians. That is what is unique to Vermeer's work; there is a sort of quiet there, encased in the painting, no matter how lovely it probably should be.

Also stolen were three Rembrandt van Rijn pieces. The Rembrandt pieces were from the 1630s when the artist was still relatively young and new in his career. In a way, that makes them all the more special. The pieces missing are *A Lady and Gentleman in Black; Christ in The Storm On The Sea of Galilee;* and *Portrait of the Artist as a Young Man* (Schwartz, 2018).

Five pieces of art by Edgar Degas, all of them on paper, were also taken. This is considered to be a big blow, as many of the pieces were of horses—something that the artist is recognized for specifically. The most important Degas piece that was stolen was the watercolor painting *Leaving the Paddock*. It is only 4-by-6 inches in size, which just makes the detail all the more impressive.

The oldest piece of art stolen by the mystery thieves is a 10-inch Chinese Gu, thought to be from around 1200 B.C.E. In 1922, it was priced at 17,500 dollars—and that price has only skyrocketed since. This Chinese Gu was also one of the oldest pieces in the museum at the time, making it all the more valuable.

Whether or not the pieces turn up somewhere is anyone's guess. The thieves managed to pull off a major heist in 1990—and today, we are still scratching our heads as to how they did it. Maybe, hopefully, one day, the pieces will be returned to the museum.

Chapter 32:

The Diving Venus

In the early 1900s, if a woman wished to go swimming, she was forced to don long, woolen garments that made movements tedious at best. It was, after all, unacceptable in society for a lady to show much of her skin. Therefore, women did not really go swimming; rather, they just sort of stood in the water, very uncomfortably.

Then, in 1905, one Annette Kellerman entered the picture. Kellerman was well known in Australia for her acting and her swimming records. Soon enough, she became known for being scandalous—and all because she invented the first one-piece swimsuit for women.

Kellerman wanted women to be able to enjoy the freedom of swimming. As she put it, "There is nothing more liberating than swimming... All life's shackles are washed away with the waves." (Smithfield, 2016) She put together what she called a figure suit—basically a very modest by today's standards one-piece swimsuit. It allowed for the freedom of movement she desperately desired, and wanted for other women as well.

Of course, it took some time for her swimsuit to catch on. In England during a trip, she had to add a pair of men's lightweight stockings to her suit in order to cover up her legs (Smithfield, 2016). When she went to Boston in America, she was even arrested for her suit showing off too much. Later, she added a sort of mini skirt panel to the suit in order to cover up some of the more controversial areas and curves of the female body.

Aside from creating the world's first one-piece swimsuit for women, Kellerman was also an accomplished actor. She starred in many movies as mermaid characters including in 1911's *The Mermaid*. In that film, in particular, she wore a functional mermaid costume that allowed her to still swim.

Later, in 1916, Kellerman became the first major actress to appear totally nude in a film (Smithfield, 2016). This film was called *A Daughter of the Gods,* which cost around one million dollars to make. That made it the most expensive film at the time. Despite the fame and success of the film, *A Daughter of the Gods* is considered to be lost media; there are no known copies left in existence.

In 1952, a film was made about Kellerman's life. It starred Esther Williams, and it was called *Million Dollar Mermaid.*

Kellerman lived to be 88 years old, passing away in November of 1975. She is still remembered as a figure of beauty and grace, as well as one of supporting women's rights.

Chapter 33:

Tulip Bubble Trouble

Today, tulip bulbs can be found at any local garden shop, or even at big retail stores—and sometimes online as well. We don't really think of them as anything special. They are so common around us that sometimes, we might not even notice the flower at all. That has not always been the case, however.

In the mid-1600s, tulip bulbs were big business.

In Holland in the 1600s, people were willing to pay top dollar for tulip bulbs. It made sense, too—back then, tulips were relatively new to the area. People came across them while trading spices along the spice routes back then. When they came to Holland, they became very popular, especially with the rich.

Soon enough, the wealthy class had gardens of tulips. They were paying a lot for garden experts to breed sturdier flowers, as the ones imported into Holland were fragile. In a bid to look wealthy, workers in the middle class of Holland soon started to covet these rare flowers as well.

It was in 1634 that "tulipmania" really gripped Holland (Hayes, 2022). During this time, tulip bulbs were selling for nearly one million dollars, if they were a rare color or pattern bloom (Hayes, 2022). Many of the mid-ranged tulip bulbs were going for much less, but still an astronomical amount of between 50,000 and 150,000 dollars a piece (Hayes, 2022). Two years later, the sales of tulips were so high that sellers had to register with the stock markets of Holland.

This could not last forever, of course. In 1637, the tulip bubble popped. Buyers could no longer afford the expensive bulbs, driving the price lower and lower and lower until it finally crashed. It should be noted that this was more of a social economical burst; the overall economy of Holland was still fine, but those with some kind of social status were not.

Today, we might consider the idea of spending fortunes on flowers foolish—but even in today's society, we have done similar things. In the 1990s and early 2000s, everyone was rushing out to purchase the newest Beanie Baby toy. Before that, it was Cabbage Patch dolls. Now, people are spending thousands upon thousands of dollars on NFTs. Truly, if there is something that is popular, there is going to be some kind of mania surrounding it—and from there, eventually, that mania's economic bubble will burst.

Chapter 34:

Cluck, Cluck, Roar!

When you look at a chicken, what do you think of? They are farmyard birds, often used for laying eggs or for their meat. Though they might peck at you when you try to pet them, they aren't really that ferocious. In fact, some of them are downright funny looking.

Yet the chicken is the closest living relative to the King of Dinosaurs—the mighty Tyrannosaurus Rex. That's right—the ancestor of the chicken you had for dinner last night might have had *you* for dinner instead!

Of course, humans and dinosaurs did not live at the same time in history. That's why we are still learning so much about them now—including what their next-of-kin are in today's world.

In 2007, scientists "managed to sequence proteins from the long-extinct creature, leading them to the discovery that many of the molecules show a remarkable similarity to those of the humble chicken" (Jha, 2007). This means that, genetically, the everyday chicken is very similar in makeup to the mighty T-Rex. According to researchers, this is the first firm indication that they have had to prove that dinosaurs and birds are actually related.

Interestingly enough, this research also proves that things like DNA and proteins do not disintegrate over time during fossilization; rather, they can remain. That means that, with time, Jurassic Park might come true. Scientists might, one day, figure out a way to clone a dinosaur.

The discovery happened in 2003 when a Tyrannosaurus Rex leg bone was recovered in the state of Montana. A paleontologist by the name of Mary Schweitzer led the team of researchers as they analyzed the bone; they were surprised to find that there was a lot of genetic material still attached to the fossil (Jha, 2007).

After it had been processed, the genetic material was found to be very similar to a modern-day chicken in structure. Some of the material was also found to be similar to proteins found in frogs and newts, though the chicken was the real winner when it came to the number of matches.

So the next time you see a chicken, remember; that small chicken has the heart and soul of a monstrous King of the dinosaurs.

Chapter 35:

To Be, or Toynbee

TOYNBEE IDEA

IN MOVIE `2001

RESURRECT DEAD

ON PLANET JUPITER

(PATOWARY, 2016)

All across the United States and South America, the above statement—or similar ones—have been found painted on mysterious tiles. They are referred to as the Toynbee Tiles. Hundreds of these tiles have been found—and yet, no one knows who is making them, or why they are being made.

What, you might ask, is Toynbee? Toynbee is thought to be a reference to Ray Bradbury's science fiction work called *The Toynbee Convector*. That story is based on the idea that, in order for mankind to survive, "it must always aim to achieve far beyond what is practically possible in order to reach something barely within reach" (PATOWARY, 2016).

It has been suggested then, that the Toynbee tiles might be suggesting that humanity must continue to progress and literally reach for the stars with ideas of colonizing places like Jupiter. This theme was explored in the film "*2001: A Space Odyssey*," which could explain the line about "the movie 2001."

The first Toynbee tile was found in Philadelphia in the 1980s. Most of the other files were found either on the East Coast of the United States or in the middle of the country, though the tiles there were fewer. A few have also been found in South America, but no one is sure if these tiles are linked to the originals, or if they are just someone else copying the idea for their own amusement.

In 1983, a man using the name James Morasco started to contact newspapers and talk shows. He claimed that he was the person responsible for creating the Toynbee tiles. He also discussed colonizing Jupiter, having come across the idea in books. The real James Morasco passed away in 2003, and apparently knew nothing about the Toynbee tiles or about colonizing Jupiter; more tiles were discovered after his death. Therefore, whoever was contacting the media in the 1980s was using that name as an alias. Throughout the years, other people claimed to have created the tiles, though none of them have been able to prove that they are actually responsible.

Perhaps the most interesting thing about the tiles is the way that they are placed. The tiles themselves are wrapped up in tar paper, and then they are placed on busy roads. Over the course of time, the tiles are pressed into the street as cars pass over them. The tar paper eventually is worn away, leaving the tile's message behind, and stamped into the road.

Chapter 36:

Ayutthaya Falls

The Kingdom of Ayutthaya was founded in the year 1350 A.D. It was located in the middle of Siam—modern-day Thailand. After four centuries, Ayutthaya fell during the Burmese-Siamese War in 1767. Today, all that remains of the once beautiful kingdom are temple ruins.

These temples were once shining beacons of the Buddhist religion and philosophy. One of these temples was the Wat Yai Chai Mongkol, which was built in 1357. This temple was originally built by the very first ruler of the Ayutthaya Kingdom—King Uthong. The Wat Yai Chai Mongkol was originally built to honor and house a sect of monks.

In modern days, the Wat Yai Chai Mongkol is still kept by monks, allowing it to be less of a ruin and more of a living temple. People are allowed to tour the buildings today. For the monks that take care of it, it is a sacred, beloved site of their religious practices.

Wat Phra Chao Phanan Choeng is another active temple within what used to be the Kingdom of Ayutthaya. It is open to any and all Buddhists for prayer. This temple actually predates the original founding of Ayutthaya itself by roughly 25 years. It also houses one of the largest statues of Buddha in all of Thailand.

One of the more popular sites to visit in Ayutthaya is that of what was once the royal palace. This area of the region is actually a part of a national historical park—the Ayutthaya Historical Park. Within the park are shops and restaurants, along with different attractions for visitors to attend. This includes elephant rides and shows with trained monkeys.

At the center of the historical park are the ruins of the royal palace, known as Wat Phra Si Sanphet. These ruins are open to the public, so anyone can visit and explore them. Though the ruins sit in, well, ruins, they are tended to and cared for by the monks that make the area their home.

A little way away from Wat Phra Si Sanphet sits the red brick, pyramid-like Wat Phra Mahathat ruins. Unfortunately, unlike the other ruins, this one was heavily damaged during the Burmese invasion years ago. There is very little left of the once grand area.

During the Burmese invasion, many of the glorious Buddha statues and figures were damaged. The monks of the time struggled to piece together the figures after the war. This left dozens of Frankensteined Buddha statues, some of them peering out from the roots of trees (Richter, 2013).

Chapter 37:

Drive-Thru Salute

It's early morning. You're running late, so you didn't have time to make yourself a hearty breakfast before heading off to work. As you drive down the road, you suddenly remember that there is a McDonald's not that far from your office—you could grab a quick bite to eat and some coffee to fuel you through that morning's meetings.

As you approach the fast food restaurant, you're relieved to notice that there is only one car ahead of you at the drive-thru. Once they've finished ordering, you ease your car up to the speaker and place your order—just something simple that you can shovel into your mouth before you punch in for the day.

This is the case for millions of Americans every day. People have many reasons for using the drive-thru, whether it be to save time or due to being sick and not wanting to go inside. In some areas, only the drive-thru is open at certain times of the day. That means if you are up late studying or if you had to pull a double shift, McDonald's is there for you, 24-7, as long as you use their drive-thru.

Yet, this was not always the case. The drive-thru as we know it was created in the 1970s when troops in Arizona were not allowed to leave their vehicles while wearing their uniforms. In order to combat this, McDonald's created areas where the troops could order from their vehicles and then be served while still inside their cars.

The original drive-thru had come earlier, back in the 1930s, but it never really caught on (Stilwell, 2022). Some other fast-food joints tried similar approaches, but it wasn't until McDonald's drive-thru for the troops that the way of ordering really became commonplace.

In May of 1999, the original McDonald's drive-thru was torn down in order to build a larger, more modern McDonald's (Stilwell, 2022). Although that drive-thru is gone, the legacy of ordering out of one's vehicle lives on, with many other restaurants and businesses taking up the same model. Even places like pharmacies and grocery stores have similar practices now, making it easier and easier for people to shop and eat whenever they want to or need to.

And all thanks to one burger joint in Arizona that wanted to feed the hungry troops stationed nearby.

Chapter 38:

Walking on Hot Stones

Fiji is a nation in the Pacific Ocean, known for its beautiful beaches and warm temperature. It is also known for being extremely welcoming to guests. This is because the Fijian people place a massive emphasis on the importance of friendship and hospitality (WorldAtlas, 2018).

Many people are surprised to learn that Fiji is not just one or a few islands, but rather, a nation of over 300 individual islands. These islands were formed thanks to volcanic activity in the past.

In Fiji, the tradition of Firewalking—walking on heated coals or stones—is very important. This tradition started around five hundred years ago by the Sawau tribe. During the Firewalking ceremony, strong men chosen from their villages will prepare by not eating coconut and by separating themselves from the female members of their villages. This is due to a legend that says if they speak with women or eat coconut before the ceremony, the stones will burn them horribly.

A pit is dug, roughly 15 feet in diameter and 4 feet deep (Captain Cook's Cruises, 2019). Large stones from nearby rivers will be collected and placed within this pit, then heated with a lot of firewood over the course of about eight hours.

The Firewalkers are then brought to the pit, surrounded by singers and dancers. Each man must make his way across the fiery stones. Once all of the men have managed to make it across the pit, a bundle of leaves and grasses are thrown into the middle of the pit, along with the leaves each man has worn around his ankles. A few days later these ashy leaves are collected, ground up, and added to water for the men to drink. Thus, the Firewalking ceremony has finished.

Why do Fijian men walk over hot stones? It's said to be a religious experience—a way to take them closer to their beliefs. For some, it is also a rite of passage, taking them from a child into manhood. Still, for others, it is a feat of strength and determination.

While Firewalking is practiced in other parts of the world, Fiji is perhaps the most well-known place for the ceremony. People come from all over the world to witness the act, partaking in days of food and fun.

Chapter 39:

Ship in a Bottle

Almost everyone has seen a ship in a bottle. These are small collectible items, usually of older ships surrounded by glass bottles. Many people marvel at how the tiny ships are built and even more wonder how the ship could get into the bottle in the first place.

Back in the 18th century, the act and art of putting miniatures into small bottles were commonplace and very popular to boot. There have been many instances of different wooden figures found in bottles, from humans and animals to ships. It is believed that this practice started with monks who painstakingly created figures and items inside of glass bottles (Super Simple, 2019).

Fast forward to the 19th century, and that's when we start to see more ships being built inside of glass bottles. This is because glass production became a bit easier during this time, allowing for clearer glass and more delicate bottles to be produced. It is said that sailors and other people who enjoyed or lived off of the sea would spend their free time building tiny ships and scenes within these bottles.

Many people used and still use the "flatpack" approach when building ships in bottles (Super Simple, 2019). This is when the ship is built, piece by piece, first outside of the bottle, then taken apart, sort of folded into itself, and then rebuilt within the bottle after being secured to some blue putty (Super Simple, 2019).

Through the 20th century, newer ships were being designed, built, and sailed on the seas, so the different models of ships available to those who put miniatures into bottles grew as well. Soon enough, people were adding in other details, such as water via the use of resin, or sculptures to show off lighthouses, mermaids, fish, and other various sea life.

In the 21st century, though the ship-in-a-bottle hobby is not as great as it used to be, there are still plenty of die-hard crafters that are enthusiastic about the hobby. Some companies even sell kits that allow you to create your own ship in a bottle by following the directions provided, similar to model car kits. These are sold online and in hobby shops all across the world.

Chapter 40:

Blimey, It's a Limey!

In the modern day, we understand that scurvy is caused by a lack of vitamin D in the human body. In the 16th century, people only understood that scurvy could be combated by the ingestion of citrus fruits—which would make sense, as citrus fruits are high in vitamin D.

Back in the 1700s, a doctor by the name of James Lind performed a controlled experiment concerning scurvy; he took twelve sailors who had scurvy and gave them different kinds of food and fruits to combat the illness. Only those that he gave citrus fruits to made a recovery (Smee, 2018).

As time passed, scurvy on the high seas started to become the number one killer of sailors—even more than storms and combat. The Royal British Navy wished to keep their men healthy; with the understanding that citrus was key in keeping scurvy out of their men, the Navy began to implement meals that included citrus fruits.

At first, the fruit of choice was the lemon, as it was easy to farm and easy to store. Later on, however, in the late 1800s, the British Navy switched to limes. This was because they believed that a single lime could fight off more scurvy than multiple lemons. We know now, however, that lemons would have been better for the sailors; limes have a tendency to lose their supply of vitamin C more quickly than a lemon does (Smee, 2018).

Because the British ships were often full of barrels of limes or lime juice, the nickname "Limey" started to become common. It then evolved into any immigrant of British descent, especially within North America, South Africa, and Australia (Smee, 2018). In modern times, Limey is often used as slang when referring to someone who is English, though it's normally done in a condescending or negative manner.

This does beg the question: If the Royal British Navy had instead packed oranges, would the Brits be called Orangeys? Or perhaps if they had stuck to lemons, they would be called Lemonies?

It should be noted that sailors also earned the nickname "Scurvy Dog" from this time period, and from the fact that many sailors got scurvy at one time or another. It would seem that the illness was the cause of many different nicknames and derogatory titles.

Thankfully, scientists have realized that fresh food and healthy meals are the best way for sailors to combat scurvy today—no more do they need to pack on barrels of limes, lemons, or oranges.

A Quick Pause...

If this book has helped you in any way, we'd appreciate it if you left us a review on Amazon. Reviews are the lifeblood of our business. We read every single one and incorporate your feedback into our future book projects.

To leave an Amazon review please visit https://www.amazon.com/ryp or scan the QR code below...THANK YOU!

Chapter 41:

Ding! Your Blood Has Been Donated!

In America, when you donate your blood, you are often thanked. Sometimes you'll receive a coupon for ice cream, be given a cookie or some chocolate, and then be sent on your merry way. In Sweden, things are a touch bit different.

You see, in Sweden, when your blood is used to help save the life of another person, you receive a text message on your cell phone, thanking you for aiding in keeping said person safe, sound, and healthy.

It is commonplace in Sweden to receive one text message after you have donated blood, and then a second one when that blood is used (Hunt, 2022). This message usually just gives thanks to the donor, letting them know that the blood is being used to save someone's life.

The practice began recently but soon gained a huge following on social media. People took to Twitter and Facebook to show off their messages, happy to have helped another human being. The idea behind sending the texts was to literally thank those that donated—but also, hopefully, urge them to come back to donate more.

Unfortunately, Sweden recently saw a dip in the amount of blood being donated within the country. Many people stopped donating, or only donated once a year, meaning that the country's blood banks were quickly being depleted.

Sweden isn't the only place that is begging for blood. Both England and America saw dips in the amount of blood donated recently as well. Sweden is the first, however, to launch the act of thanking people for their donations via text. The hope is to spread the word via social media—which has happened so far—and to bring in other potential donors.

In fact, in Sweden, there are some areas that ask people to sign a contract that allows the blood banks to text them relentlessly until that person has given blood again. This tactic seems to be working on some people. Upon seeing this tactic, England adopted something similar. Now, on June 14th, which is World Blood Donor Day, all donors, new and old, will receive a text message reminding them to give blood (Hunt, 2022).

One can only wonder how long it will take for America to adopt a similar text reward and reminder.

Chapter 42:

The Mystery of the Babushka Lady

The day was November 22nd, 1963. In Dallas, Texas, scores of people were happily waiting to watch the presidential motorcade pass by. It was a thrilling experience; people wanted to see President John F. Kennedy in person.

That day would go down in American history as one of the darkest days ever. That was the day that the President of the United States was assassinated.

The people on the streets during the assassination were later identified, either by their legal names or by identifying nicknames, such as the Umbrella Man or the Badge Man (Raga, 2016). Among these people was the woman that would come to be known as the Babushka Lady.

This mystery woman was wearing what appeared to be a headscarf, similar to a Russian Babushka, when her picture was taken on November 22nd. Photographic documents show that she was standing in the grass between Main Street and Elm Street, photographing the location where John F. Kennedy was shot (Raga, 2016). Although many people through the years have been interviewed about this woman, no one knows, even today, who she was. The footage of the assassination that she might have captured has disappeared, too, meaning that any evidence she might have accidentally captured is missing.

The day that John F. Kennedy was shot, many people had cameras at the ready. They wanted to have photographs to mark the day that they saw the President in person—and many of these photographs caught the unfortunate events that ended up playing out. In many of these photographs and crude films taken that day, the Babushka Lady appeared.

One of these short pieces of film catches the Babushka Lady just after the assassination, standing close to where the president lost his life. She is seen facing the grassy knoll. What's odd about this is that, while the people around her are panicking and running around, she is simply standing there, watching, with apparently no fear or worry.

Seven years later, the dancer Beverly Oliver claimed that she was the Babushka Lady. This was later debunked, as her story seemed to be one made up more for fame than anything else.

So who was the Babushka Lady, really? Some people think that she might have been a Russian spy, there on the day of the assassination to capture footage of the president's murder. Others claim that she was a secondary shooter, there to take out anyone that got in the way of the assassination. Still, others think that she was a man in a dress, perhaps working with the shooter. If she had been taking photographs or film of the scene in front of her, she would have been able to take pictures of the grassy knoll, meaning that she would have evidence of a secondary shooter.

Whatever the case, she never came forward to the police. Any evidence she might have had is lost now—and it is very possible that we will never know the true identity of the Babushka Lady.

Chapter 43:

Teeny Tiny House of Law

In Carrabelle, Florida, the world's smallest police station is, very simply, a phone booth.

This tiny station came into existence in 1963 on March 10th. Apparently, the city of Carrabelle in Florida had been having issues with its tourists. The tourists would make unauthorized, long-distance calls on the police telephone (Carrabelle City Hall Office Complex, 2022). This phone was a part of a call box that was very literally attached to a building.

According to the Carrabelle, Florida's website, "Johnnie Mirabella, St. Joe Telephone's lone Carrabelle employee at the time, first tried moving the call box to another building, but the illegal calls continued" (Carrabelle City Hall Office Complex, 2022). Mirabella later realized that the police were using the telephone in the rain, thus soaking themselves. When a nearby store was getting rid of its phone booth, Mirabella asked for it so that he could protect the officers from the rain.

With help from another officer, Mirabella moved the police telephone to its new home—U.S. 98, under a chinaberry tree (Carrabelle City Hall Office Complex,

2022). Though this solved the issue of officers getting wet on rainy days, tourists still felt the urge to use the phone to make calls out of state. Later on, the telephone's dial was removed, making it impossible for the tourists to use it while still allowing functionality for the police officers.

This phone booth is technically the smallest police station in the world. It has gained some fame since it was first installed, having been featured in newspaper articles, magazines, and even television shows. Some of the shows it has been featured on include *Ripley's Believe it or Not!, Real People,* and *The Today Show.* It was even featured in a movie called *Tate's Hell.*

Visitors are even able to walk away with some paraphernalia featuring the teeny, tiny police station. There are shirts and hats available to be purchased, as well as calendars and postcards, all of them featuring the phone booth.

Of course, fame comes with a price—the poor little police station has been vandalized multiple times, some even going so far as to shoot it. It has also been knocked over on a few occasions, both by truck and by hurricane. A tourist was so enamored with the thing that he tried to load the phone booth into the back of his pickup truck, hoping to take it home with him!

Chapter 44:

All That Glitters Is Gold

There is an asteroid that some people call the Golden Asteroid. This chunk of rock is better known as Psyche 16, named after the Greek Goddess of the soul. It is thought to contain a massive amount of gold, as well as other precious metals. That is one of the major reasons why scientists wish to probe it.

Originally, the asteroid was set to be probed in 2022. However, due to issues with some of the software needed to probe the asteroid, the launch date has been pushed back to as late as 2024—if the launch flies at all. There is a very large worry that the probe will never leave the Earth, as the cost of sending it to explore Psyche 16 continues to grow.

One of the main reasons that scientists hope to get to Psyche 16 is that, according to NASA, the asteroid has "… the partial core of a shattered planetesimal—a small world the size of a city or small country that is the first building block of a planet. If it is, asteroid Psyche can offer a close look at the interior of terrestrial planets like Earth that are normally hidden beneath layers of mantle and crust" (Whittington, 2022). Simply put, by exploring and studying the asteroid, scientists might be able to gain more information as to how planets like Earth are formed.

Currently, there are two schools of thought as to what the asteroid is made up of. Most scientists can agree that there are precious metals on and in Psyche 16; it's the amount of these metals that they cannot yet agree on.

Some people believe that the asteroid is a solid chunk of precious metals, mostly gold. If they are correct, then the monetary worth of the asteroid is in the quintillions—enough money to make just about everyone on Earth a billionaire. Some people have even estimated as high as 700 quintillion dollars, which is a very large chunk of change (Whittington, 2022).

As exciting as that amount of money is, most scientists now believe that the golden asteroid is actually only gold plated—that is, it is a structure that is surrounded by precious metals with a less dense center. This would lessen the overall monetary value of the asteroid to around 11 trillion—which is still a lot of money.

Either way, pro-space mining groups are getting ready. As long as Psyche 16 is probed, then people will be dreaming of all of the gold they can mine from the asteroid. This is a relatively new method of mining—it was considered science fiction for so long. Now, with the study of the golden asteroid, space mining might just become science's future.

Chapter 45:

He Wants YOU for the US Army

During World War I, one of the most iconic enlisting campaigns in the history of the United States was out in full force. Every street held spectacular posters featuring a characterization of the United States as Uncle Sam—almost a mascot for the country at the time. These posters featured him pointing at the viewer, words around him declaring that he "Wants YOU for the US Army."

This iconic poster was painted and designed by James Montgomery Flagg, a well-known and famous illustrator of the time. It was originally used as a means to promote preparedness for the households of the United States but was later adapted by the US Army as a way of stirring patriotism in the hearts and minds of young men. Well over 4 million copies of it were printed during the course of WWI (Knauer, 2017).

As iconic as Uncle Sam is, what do we really know about him? How did he come to be the sort of mascot for the United States? From what we know, "Uncle Sam" might have been an actual man—one Sam Wilson, a meat packer known for stamping his barrels of meat with "U.S." during the War of 1812 (Knauer, 2017).

It wasn't until the mid-19th century that the Uncle Sam we know today appeared. In the design he is most recognized as, he is a long and lean, caucasian man with a white or gray goatee. He is often seen in a tall hat emblazoned with stars and stripes, and he is usually wearing an American flag-themed suit. Uncle Sam usually has a very stern, no-nonsense look about him, his face very stern. This look was adopted by and adapted by Thomas Nast in 1877.

America wasn't the only one using this sort of tactic to get recruits. In 1914, British artist Alfred Leete drew up a poster of famed hero Lord Kitchener pointing at the viewer. This poster was then used by Flagg when he decided to draw up one for the United States. Flagg based his version of Uncle Sam loosely off of this poster (Knauer, 2017).

The face of Uncle Sam, however—at least in Flagg's illustration—was based off of the artist's own image.

However it came into being, the poster that Flagg created quickly became iconic in the United States—and soon enough, the world over.

Chapter 46:

The Deaths of Rap Legends

In the 1990s, there were two major names in rap music; Biggie Smalls—also known as the Notorious B.I.G.—and Tupac Shakur. Then, tragedy—in 1996, at the age of 25, Tupac was shot and killed during a drive-by shooting. Less than a year later, Christopher Wallace (Biggie Smalls's real name) was gunned down as well. Biggie was only 24 years old.

Yet, today, almost 30 years later, no one knows who killed them, or if their deaths were related. There is plenty of speculation and plenty of theories, but as of right now, the public does not know the truth. The sad fact is that we probably never will.

However, some people still have possible theories as to who was responsible for the murder of these two rap legends. Many people believe that, at least in Biggie's case, the shooter might have been a corrupt cop or a hired hitman (Crime Feed Staff, 2022). Still, others believe that both Tupac and Biggie were killed by the same person—someone who wanted them both out of the picture for one reason or another.

The people who believe Biggie's death to have been caused by a corrupt police officer include the rapper's mother and family members. In 2002, she filed a wrongful death lawsuit against the Los Angeles Police Department (Crime Feed Staff, 2022). This was followed up by a judge finding that the police department had withheld important information and evidence. In 2005, said judge made the police department pay 1 million dollars to Biggie's estate for damages and legal fees. In 2007, the family again brought up a suit against the Los Angeles Police Department, claiming that there had been a conspiracy against the rapper. This case was later thrown out by a judge (Crime Feed Staff, 2022).

Still others suspect that Biggie's death was caused by his feud with Tupac—and that Tupac's death was caused by the same feud.

Originally, the two rappers were very good friends. Over time, however, they grew to become rivals. In November of 1994, Tupac was shot five times. He survived but blamed the shooting on Biggie and Biggie's friends. Around two months later, Biggie released a track called "Who Shot Ya?", which seemed to have been aimed at Tupac. Tupac took this as a blow—though the song was probably written prior to the attack.

In return, Tupac released a track called "Hit 'Em Up," in which he claimed that he had an affair with Biggie Smalls's wife, Faith Evans. Evans denied having ever been in the alleged affair, but the song nonetheless made Biggie's blood boil.

After Tupac's murder, Biggie Smalls claimed that he had nothing to do with the attack. Only a few months later, however, he fell to a similar fate. It ended the feud between the two rappers, but their mysterious deaths would soon go down in history as tragedies.

Chapter 47:

The Power of Marigolds

Snakes might be fearsome to some and cute to others, but most people can agree: If they are venomous, you do not want them in your garden or around your house. There are numerous types of plants that help to naturally repel snakes.

Areas of lush plant cover will attract mice and other rodents, which in turn attract snakes. That is why it is important to make sure your gardens incorporate some kind of snake-repelling plant or flower. Whether it is a vegetable garden or a flower garden, there are many different kinds of plants that will keep you and your loved ones safe.

You should keep in mind that not all plants and flowers flourish in every environment. So, while some plants might work best for some areas of the world, other plants might die right away.

Perhaps the most important thing to note about snake-repelling plants for your gardens is that the flowers and plants used are actually more likely to repel the snake's food source—that being small mammals like mice and rats. These rodents are bad for your garden as well, often eating up your plants. Keeping your garden rodent-free will also keep it snake-free.

The most useful and popular plant to use to repel snakes and rodents is the humble marigold. This is due to the plant's roots (k2forma, 2018). The roots are thick, going deep into the earth, and give off a horrible odor. Many common pests, like gophers and chipmunks, hate the smell of the roots. By keeping those rodents away, you will also be keeping snakes away.

The second best plant for deterring rodents and snakes is the Mother-In-Law's Tongue. This plant actually repels snakes, straight up, without the need to deter rodents. Because of this, it is a good idea to use it in conjunction with other repellants. The leaves of a Mother-In-Law's Tongue are sharp and dangerous for snakes to brush up against. Because of that, they will steer clear of the plant altogether.

If you are growing a vegetable garden, consider growing onions and garlic. Like Mother-In-Law's Tongue, these are both deterrents to snakes specifically. Both onions and garlic give off an odor that snakes dislike. What's more, garlic plants produce an oil that, when it comes into contact with a snake's skin and scales, produces a dizzying, disorientating effect—similar to pepper spray to a human (k2forma, 2018).

The best way to repel a snake from your garden is to use one of these plants in conjunction with another. If your climate allows it, having at least two is a great start to keeping you and your garden safe from potentially venomous snakes.

Chapter 48:

Che Guevara Was... Irish?

Che Guevara was a prominent figure during the Cuban Revolution. He spread communist ideas throughout the nation, taking to fighting in guerilla warfare during the revolution's peak. In 1967, he was executed by the Bolivian army (Davidson, 2021).

Today, Che Guevara is remembered as an icon of resistance. People celebrate him and his ideals of leftist radicalism and anti-imperialism (Davidson, 2021). A famous picture of him is now used across the world on t-shirts and posters, idolizing him for his beliefs.

There is much more to Che Guevara than meets the eye, however. Many tend to forget that he was a loyal and loving father, a poetry lover, a chess fanatic, and a doctor (Davidson, 2021).

For example, Che Guevara was not his real name. The name "Che" was a type of greeting, similar to saying "hey there, guy," or "mate." Apparently, because he used it so frequently when speaking with his compatriots, they started to call him by it. His full name was recorded as Ernesto Rafael Guevara de la Serna.

Furthermore, Che Guevara came from Irish ancestry. Patrick Lynch immigrated to Argentina from Ireland in the 1700s. Lynch was Che Guevara's great-great-great-great grandfather, and many attributed Lynch's Irish blood to fueling Che's rebellious nature.

Because Che Guevara suffered from asthma, he was unable to play his beloved rugby as often as he wanted to. He ended up taking up chess to fill his time. He also started to study medicine due to his condition. It piqued an interest in the medical field, which in turn led to him becoming a doctor. Specifically, he studied leprosy and allergies.

Che was also a family man. He married Hilda Gadea in 1955 after she revealed that she was pregnant with Che's child (Davidson, 2021). Unfortunately, this marriage ended in a divorce, with Che going on to marry Aledia March, a fellow revolutionary. Together, the pair had four children.

One of Che's children, named Aleida, once remarked, "my father knew how to love, and that was the most beautiful feature of him—his capacity to love. To be a proper revolutionary, you have to be a romantic. His capacity to give himself to the cause of others was at the center of his beliefs. If we could only follow his example,

the world would be a much more beautiful place"
(Davidson, 2021).

"Guerrillero Heroico" is considered to be the most
famous picture of Che Guevara. It has also been
considered the most famous picture of all time by The
Maryland Institute of Art (Davidson, 2021). This
photograph was taken in 1960, and soon enough went
on to emblazon thousands of t-shirts, posters, and even
stamps.

Chapter 49:

The Rainbow River

In Colombia, there is a river that runs with different colors. It is known as The Rainbow River or the Caño Cristales River. This river appears to be loads of different colors—the colors of a rainbow.

This is caused by the growth of an aquatic plant known as *Macarenia clavigera;* this plant only grows within the confines of the river itself (McConnaughhay, 2022). The makeup of these plants, along with minerals found in the river, plus the way that the sun hits said plants, makes the *Macarenia clavigera* turn vibrant shades of purple, red, and green. Depending on the time of year, these plants might also appear orange or pink.

The colors are so beautiful and awe-inspiring that the locals claim that the river is a remnant of the Garden of Eden, a lush garden from Biblical stories. Some claim that the river has five colors, while others claim that there are up to seven.

The river is so famous that it was recently featured in the Disney film *Encanto,* and it has been featured in the National Geographic magazine as one of the most colorful destinations on Earth (McConnaughhay, 2022).

The Caño Cristales River can be found in the Serranía de la Macarena, which is close to the town of La Macarena in Columbia. It is in the middle of a national park. Aside from the nearby town, the area is mostly untouched by mankind, leaving it natural and beautiful. Many people like to hike in the area or along the river itself, taking plenty of pictures.

Tourists generally try to visit the Rainbow River between the months of July and November. This is when the colors of the river are considered to be the most vibrant and beautiful. During the rest of the year, the plants in the water are not in bloom, so the colors are either muted or nonexistent.

If you are planning a vacation to see the Rainbow River, remember that there are plenty of other destinations nearby, too. The river itself is beautiful and very picturesque, but there are also a lot of hiking trails that lead to secret waterfalls and other areas of the river that, while not as colorful, are just as beautiful.

Remember, too, that there are some areas of the river that are extremely colorful, while other parts of the river are a bit more muted. It all depends on how much sunlight the aquatic plants are getting and the time of the year. Either way—make sure you bring a camera!

Chapter 50:

The Speed of Sound

In October of 1997, one car burst through the sound barrier and into the history books. That car was the Thrust SSC, also known as the Thrust SuperSonic Car. It sped along the desert in Nevada at the speed of 763 miles per hour.

This vehicle was driven by Andrew Green, a retired British Air Force Pilot. Of Green's ride, the Guinness Book of World Records stated, "The two huge booms that rang out over the site during Andy's outward and return run sent his crew into spontaneous cheers— though because he was actually inside the vehicle that caused those sonic booms, he couldn't hear them himself... Green had driven faster than any other person in history...his record-breaking ride came 50 years and one day after the sound barrier was first broken, by Chuck Yeager (USA) in a rocket plane, the Bell X-1. So the letters 'SSC' in the car's name proved prophetic after all: They stood for 'SuperSonic Car'" (Papadopoulos, 2022).

The Thrust SSC is now on display in Coventry, England, at a museum for transportation. It can be viewed by the public. Though it is not on the road today, it is considered to be a marvel of vehicle engineering.

For example, the Thrust SSC is run by two engines that are generally used in McDonnell Douglas F-4 Phantom II jets (Papadopoulos, 2022). It weighs almost 10 tons, and it is very large—spanning 54 ft long.

When the vehicle was being used by Green, it accelerated roughly 25 miles per hour per second (Papadopoulos, 2022). During that ride, Green reported that the car was just about uncontrollable, with the wheels wanting to turn to the left. When it was time to stop the car, the Thrust SSC had to deploy parachutes in order to slow down—no real braking system would work on a car going that fast.

In 2016, the Thrust SSC was supposed to be taken out of retirement in order to be driven again. Unfortunately, it seems that Green was not up to the task for a second time. The car is still viewable at the museum in Coventry—but maybe one day in the near future, its tires will hit the sandy desert road in Nevada once again.

Chapter 51:

Scarface

Many people have heard the name Al Capone. Many have heard his nickname Scarface, mostly in thanks to the famous film about his life. Yet few people know the entire history of the man. Where did he get the nickname? Who was he, really? Where did he grow up?

That last question is maybe the easiest to answer. Though he was well known for the mafia in Chicago, Al Capone actually grew up in New York. His parents were immigrants, and his mother gave birth to him in 1899. Capone was just one in a family of nine children. Though the Capone family might have been happy, they were very poor. Some have speculated that growing up without a lot of necessities might have led Capone to look for something better in life.

In middle school, Al Capone started to lose interest in academics (Hughes, 2021). Instead, he started to hang out with the wrong sort of people, which only hastened his climb into the criminal underworld. Prior to that, he had been a very good student. That was until he hit one of his teachers. From then on, he never stepped foot in a school to learn again.

Instead, Capone took a variety of odd jobs in order to support himself. He also started to join different gangs, including the South Brooklyn Rippers, Forty Thieves Juniors, and the James Street Boys (Hughes, 2021). These were not big-time gangs, however; mostly, they were just groups of young boys and young men that would shoplift or vandalize local businesses.

While working at a club as a bartender, Capone got into a fight with one of the patrons. During the fight, he was struck across the face with a sharp object, thus receiving the scar that would lead to his famous nickname— Scarface.

Shortly after the fight, Capone relocated to Chicago. This was in 1920. While in Chicago, Capone worked with many shady businessmen. He amassed a wealth of money, eventually purchasing a home in Florida. It is believed that he was responsible for the St. Valentine's Day Massacre, when a group of mobsters from a rival gang were assassinated, having orchestrated the event from his home.

Capone denied any and all involvement with the massacre, despite what the police and rival gangs thought. He was also a mastermind behind a lot of crime in both Chicago and Miami, Florida. Because of this, the police were looking for any reason to throw him in jail.

Eventually, they got their chance—Capone was arrested, tried, and imprisoned for tax evasion. For his crime, he received an eleven-year sentence—part of which he served out in the famed Alcatraz prison (Hughes, 2021).

Capone passed away in 1947 due to complications of dementia and due to an infection, he had suffered during his time in prison.

Chapter 52:

Wow!

In the summer of 1977, Jerry Ehman might have become the first person to receive an intentional message from outer space while he was volunteering for SETI (Nelson, 2019). SETI is short for the Search for Extraterrestrial Intelligence. Ehman was scanning different radio signals that were coming from deep space (Nelson, 2019).

While scanning the signals, Ehman saw his equipment spike. The message that he received lasted for 72 seconds and seemed to have come from the Sagittarius constellation. That's over 120 light years away from Earth.

Ehman's equipment recorded the signal, and when the signal's information was printed out, Ehman wrote "wow!" on the paper. That is why this signal is now called the Wow! Signal.

So what did the signal say? Very simply put, the signal was read as "6EQUJ5." According to the writer Michael Brooks, "The letters and numbers are, essentially, a measure of the intensity of the electromagnetic signal as it hits the receiver. Low power was recorded with numbers 0 to 9; as power got higher, the computer used letters: 10 was A, 11 was B and so on" (KRULWICH, 2010). This means that the signal was extremely strong, as indicated by the letter "U" in the readout.

The reading of "U" is, indeed, very loud. It is roughly 30 times louder than anything else having been recorded previously from deep space. The thought is that a signal that loud must have been sent by something or someone with powerful equipment—possibly aliens attempting to contact other life forms.

This would explain Ehman's reaction of "Wow!" The major problem, though, was where exactly the signal had come from. As stated previously, the signal seemed to have come from the Sagittarius constellation—but the problem was that there is no star there, nor any planet that we are aware of.

Another suggested issue is that we do not know everything there is to know about deep space yet. It is possible that the sound was not a signal at all, but rather, something making a very loud noise in space that we are not aware of. For example, when black holes collide, they make a very loud sound that can come across as a signal. If this is the case, it would explain why there have not been any other signals from that area since that fateful day in 1977.

Still, it is possible that the Wow! Signal was, indeed, a signal from beyond the stars. It is possible that it has repeated before, but scientists were simply unable to record the sound again. Hopefully, time will tell whether or not Ehman caught the sound of an alien species trying to contact us—or not.

Chapter 53:

The Birth of Reggae

Reggae is probably the most recognizable genre of music to have come out of Jamaica. It started to gain popularity in the 1960s, though its roots can be traced back further than that.

Predating the popularity of reggae music were the styles of *mento*—a rural style of music that had formed during slavery, and ska (Homiak, 2021). Ska evolved from a combination of *mento* and rhythm and blues, the latter of which became a popular musical import from North America. Soon enough, jazz was added to the ska equation, creating an entirely new genre of music.

Evolving further from ska came reggae. A lot of popular ska artists during the 1950s and 1960s made the switch over to the new form of music, including Bob Marley, Peter Tosh and Bunny Wailer, and the Wailers. Ska started to slow down, incorporating more drum beats and fewer horns. This is when reggae appeared in its infancy.

Reggae appeared as its own genre in 1968, focusing on slower beats and lyrics concerning slavery and the exploitation of black culture in popular media of the time. Most importantly, reggae was a reflection of the cultural and political atmosphere of Jamaica at the time.

You see, previously, the black communities in Jamaica had been denied any sort of approval from Africa concerning their heritages. The Rastafarian movement was very proud of their African roots and wanted Jamaicans to be treated with respect and honor. In 1966, they received that honor from the Emperor of Ethiopia.

The Emperor paid a visit to Jamaica and was so moved by the people there that he ended up awarding thirteen gold medals to Rustifarian leaders in Jamaica, citing their work for the Pan-African people.

Since then, reggae has been seen as and treated as a celebration of African culture through the sound and beat of the music itself, combining traditional African beats with popular, modern music of the time.

Nowadays, reggae is shared and enjoyed all over the world.

Chapter 54:

The Gold of Oak Island

Located off of the coast of Nova Scotia in Canada lies Oak Island. This unassuming little island is host to one of the most interesting pirate-related mysteries of all time. Supposedly, the pirate captain William Kidd buried a massive amount of gold and jewels on the island in a pit.

For hundreds of years, people have traveled to Oak Island in an attempt to find the hidden money. Many historians and treasure hunters believe that this famed pit is located on the eastern side of Oak Island. According to the local lore, a teenager in 1795, along with his friends, discovered a massive shaft complete with wooden structures for people to climb on (Homer, 2020).

Unfortunately, the shaft was soon filled in due to storms and the tide, burying it once again. Since the 1960s, numerous indentations on the shore have been dug up in the hopes of rediscovering this famed money pit. Explorers have found booby traps as well, keeping them from finding the money pit again—including a tunnel that fills different areas of the island with water from the ocean (Homer, 2020).

Although the most plausible theory as to what is buried in that pit seems to center around Captain Kidd's plundering of a Spanish galleon, there are other theories that the treasure in the pit might be a bit more holy. Some historians believe that the treasure on the island did not come from Captain Kidd, but rather, from the Knights Templar—possibly even the Holy Grail itself.

To add fuel to the fire, there have already been a few, small treasures discovered on Oak Island. They include pieces of old china, parchment, a lead cross, and drill bits dipped in gold (Homer, 2020). Most of these treasures are not worth a lot when it comes to money, but historically, they are worth a fortune in themselves.

Perhaps the most interesting pieces that have been found on the island include 16th-century coins and a gold chain (Homer, 2020). A stone was also found, bearing text that does not appear to be in any known language. The text on this stone might in fact be some kind of cipher, and many treasure hunters believe that if they figure out the code, they will find the money pit.

There have been a few attempts at translating the text. The most notable translation reads, "FORTY FEET BELOW TWO MILLION POUNDS ARE BURIED"

(Homer, 2020). Still, others believe that the code has not been cracked, and is rather something left behind by Holy Knights when they buried the Holy Grail.

If you are interested in the history and lore of Oak Island, there are weekend tours available. Maybe you will be the one to find the money pit of Oak Island!

Chapter 55:

Did Robin Hood Exist?

Just about everyone knows about Robin Hood. He is a dashing thief who takes from the rich to give to the poor of England. There have been many films, television shows, books, and other media surrounding the famed hero thief.

The stories of Robin Hood date back to the 15th century—and possibly beforehand as well—with plays and games celebrating May Day that involved a very Robin Hood-like figure (History Channel Editors, 2010). Later, in the 19th century, writers like Howard Pyle would create fantastic stories surrounding Robin Hood, making him a household name far beyond the reaches of England (History Channel Editors, 2010).

It seems that no matter the time, some kind of Robin Hood figure has existed. Sometimes this person is a skilled assassin with a good heart, going after crooked government workers. Other times, he is a gentleman thief, using the money he stole to make better the lives of the less fortunate. No matter what kind of story he is in, he is always some kind of hero to the unfortunate and needy, and a bitter enemy of those who hold power over those people.

Where did the original Robin Hood come from? Surely there must have been some historical figure that we can point at to show that a man like this existed at one point. According to historians, the name Robin Hood very well may have originated with the term *Robehod* in the 13th century. This was a term used for criminals of that time period, meaning that the name Robin Hood is just an evolution of a slang term.

Robin Hood himself, as a character, first appeared in ballads in the 14th century (Countryfile Magazine, 2022). These ballads claim that Robin Hood was a master of disguising himself and that he lived out his life with his merry band of men.

Despite this, it is still very possible that a person existed that ended up becoming the starting point for the Robin Hood legends. Many historians who have studied medieval times believe that a Robin Hood-like figure might have existed in the 12th or 13th century, though no one is quite sure exactly where he might have lived.

The first written instance of a living, breathing version of Robin Hood came about in 1377. This was in *The Vision of Piers Ploughman* by William Langland, though it should be noted that the surname of Robinhood existed as far back as Henry the III's rule—though it appears that it was usually a nickname given to thieves (Countryfile Magazine, 2022).

There is one common theory for who the real Robin Hood may have been. That would be the Earl of Huntington, who passed away in 1198 (Countryfile Magazine, 2022). As evidence, there is a grave in Yorkshire, specifically in Kirklees Hall, that reads: "Here underneath this little stone / Lies Robert Earl of Huntington / Never archer there as he so good / And people called him Robin Hood / Such outlaws as him and his men / Will England never see again" (Countryfile Magazine, 2022).

For now, we have to be content with all of the stories about the famed Robin Hood. Maybe one day, a text will be found that reveals the truth about this nobel thief—or, perhaps, it is more fun to simply imagine what kind of mischief Robin Hood could get up to.

Chapter 56:

The Hero Admiral

Yi Sun-shin, sometimes known as Yi Sun-sin, was born in what is now South Korea in the year 1545. He is considered a hero in his home country and is famous for having repelled invading Japanese forces during the 1590s (The Editors of the Encyclopaedia Britannica, 2019).

In 1576, Yi Sun-shin became a military officer and was promoted in 1591 to the commander of the naval forces. He was then stationed in the Left Chŏlla province. While there, he focused on training these troops and developing what might have been the very first iron-sided battleship, the *kŏbuksŏn*—translated as the turtle ship.

The *kŏbuksŏn* was renowned for having massive armored plates used to protect the men aboard the ship, along with numerous spikes and knives attached to its hull to keep enemy forces from scaling the ship to board. Furthermore, this ship had a dragon's head for the bow, which was equipped with a cannon. Other cannons were stationed around the ship, and the smoke from these firearms would be used to mask the ship's location. It was a fearsome creation, to be sure.

In 1592, while the rest of the Korean military was not ready, Yi Sun-shin's men were. The Japanese suddenly attacked. Initially, the Japanese had the upper hand— but because of Yi Sun-shin and his troops cutting off their supplies, the Japanese invaders quickly fell and retreated (The Editors of the Encyclopaedia Britannica, 2019).

For his efforts, Yi Sun-shin was given control of the entire Korean naval fleet, but in 1597, he was falsely accused of disloyalty (The Editors of the Encyclopaedia Britannica, 2019). Because of this, he was demoted to a lowly, common soldier. Shortly thereafter, the Japanese invaded for a second time, and without Yi Sun-shin to lead the navy, the Japanese army was able to defeat the Korean forces.

During this second invasion, the Korean military leaders realized that the only way they were going to stop Japan from successfully taking over the country was to reinstate Yi Sun-shin as the head of the navy. Taking the men that were left, along with the few boats, he was able to fight back against the Japanese fighters, taking back the Korean seas.

During one of these battles to reclaim Korean waters, Yi Sun-shin was killed when a bullet pierced him. His men continued to fight on, keeping their country safe from the Japanese invaders.

Yi Sun-shin went down in Korean history as a hero of war. Without him, South Korea as we know it today might not have existed.

Chapter 57:

Voodoo Queen

In the 19th century, New Orleans was mesmerized by one Marie Laveau—a voodoo priestess. While she was called a satanic cultist by white society during her time, was Marie Laveau really a horrible, magical cultist? The short answer—no. In fact, to the black society of the time, she was a healer with practices rooted firmly in African culture.

Every Sunday in Congo Square in New Orleans, Louisiana, Marie Laveau would hold healing ceremonies that centered around her faith. Congo Square was an important meeting place for the black community at the time, as they were not allowed in white spaces. Here, at the square, the black community could gather.

Because the ceremonies that Marie Laveau practiced were different from white church meetings, the while folk of the time decided that Laveau must have been an occultist, and claimed that her ceremonies were just drunken fits of devil worship (Dimuro, 2018).

Unfortunately, that view of Laveau and her faith has persisted over time, with people even today considering her some kind of practitioner of black magic. The truth is much richer than any horrible story one could fathom.

Around 1801, Laveau was born—her exact date of birth is unknown to historians. Her mother was a freed slave, while her father was a businessman. When she grew older, Laveau developed a relationship with a white man—Captain Christophe Dominique Glapion.

Laveau and Glapion lived together for roughly 30 years, and they had multiple children together. However, due to the laws of the time, they were not legally allowed to be married. During her time with Glapion, Laveau was very popular with merchants and lawyers, offering her opinion on legal matters and current events (Dimuro, 2018). She was also well known for aiding the sick.

All throughout this time, Laveau was also known for holding ceremonies in her home on Fridays. These ceremonies were ones of healing and the Voodoo faith, earning her the title of Voodoo Queen and the Voodoo Priestess of New Orleans.

Unfortunately, many white folk of the time did not think of Voodoo as a proper religion; instead, they claimed that it was the study and worship of the devil. They saw it as something to oppose Christianity, so they thought of it as black magic. Many of those who witnessed the Voodoo ceremonies—which included chanting and dancing—later told others that the ceremonies were meant to summon devils and demons, or to steal souls. Because of this, Voodoo gained a reputation of negativity—one that still, unfortunately, remains today.

Aside from being the famed Voodoo Priestess of New Orleans, Laveau was also known to aid in the care of yellow fever victims. She was also an advocate for black women's rights, often posting bail for women who were jailed wrongfully (Dimuro, 2018). She was also known to speak with and pray with inmates on death row.

Laveau passed away in June of 1881. While many people celebrated her life, there were many others that cursed her. To this day, she is a widely controversial person, with some seeing her as a healer, and others seeing her as a Queen of dark magic. People in New Orleans will travel to her gravesite to ask for blessings, often leaving behind little trinkets.

Hopefully, this beloved Voodoo Queen can help those from beyond the grave—just as she helped those during her life.

Chapter 58:

Springtime on Mars

In March, it is officially springtime on Mars—and you know what that means! The mysterious polygons on the planet's surface have gone white! Recorded in 2022, these polygons are large, white lines that make up a sort of patchwork design on the surface of the Red Planet (Specktor, 2022).

According to the University of Arizona, "Both water and dry ice have a major role in sculpting Mars' surface at high latitudes... Water ice frozen in the soil splits the ground into polygons" (Specktor, 2022). This means that those odd shapes are actually something that happens every year around the springtime. They are completely normal for Mars.

As the frozen ice hits the surface of Mars and melts into a gas, vents are created. These vents hold dry ice. This act leaves fan-shaped, dark particle deposits along the surface of the planet. These vents can open and close numerous times during the spring (Specktor, 2022). The different winds on Mars can spread the particles pushed to the surface via the vents in different directions, which is why there are both dark lines and lighter lines visible on the surface (Specktor, 2022).

The photographs showing this process rode on NASA's Mars Reconnaissance Orbiter. This orbiter was launched in 2006 and has since captured many unique and interesting photographs of the Red Planet.

Another interesting set of photographs captured by the Mars Reconnaissance Orbiter includes pictures of what is thought to be the largest canyon found in our solar system. This canyon, dubbed the Valles Marineris, is roughly 10 times longer than our own Grand Canyon, here on Earth. The Valles Marineris is thought to be around three times deeper than our Grand Canyon as well—making it a massive formation (Specktor, 2022).

As the years pass and we are able to get better glimpses of our surrounding planets, we learn more and more about how planets were formed. Earth is but a speck against the backdrop of outer space; the more we learn about the universe around us, the more questions we find ourselves asking.

At least, for now, we understand why there are patchwork-like polygons on the surface of Mars during the spring.

Chapter 59:

The Mystery of the Franklin Expedition

In the year 1845, the famed English explorer Sir John Franklin sailed to Canada. With him, he had two heated ships and a large crew, as well as enough food to last the entire expedition for three years. Franklin and his crew set off in the hopes of finding a trade route through the Arctic—one that would be easy to sail and that would connect the Atlantic Ocean to the Pacific Ocean.

Franklin and his crew were never seen again.

In the years that followed, over 30 other expeditions struck out with the hopes of finding the lost crew and their leader. All of these ended in failure, and worse—many of the crew members of these expeditions lost their lives in the process. In fact, so many people on rescue missions died that their total number succeeded the number of crewmen on Franklin's expedition.

After many years of searching, some evidence finally appeared in 1859. The skeletal remains of a human were found beside a log book or diary. The last entry in this journal was in April of 1848 (Kiger, 2015).

According to the journal that was found, Franklin's two ships became stuck in the thick ice of the tundra. The crew members tried to free the ships, but after two years, 23 members of the crew, along with Franklin himself, had passed away. Those that remained decided to abandon the ships, taking off on foot across the tundra in hopes of finding civilization.

Surely, you must be thinking, these men died from the cold conditions, or from starvation. You would be wrong. In the 1980s, researchers and historians decided that most of the men on Franklin's crew probably died of tuberculosis and similar diseases. This is because the canned food they had eaten from the ships' stores were full of lead from the cans. The food poisoning weakened the crew, leaving them as open targets to all different kinds of diseases.

Added to the lead poisoning, the crew was very ill-equipped to travel across the tundra. They had expected to remain on the ships, heated and safe, during their journey. Instead, thrust out onto the ice and into the cold, they were literally sitting ducks.

Chapter 60:

Boats Under San Francisco

During the height of the gold excitement, there were at least five hundred ships stranded in the harbor, some without even a watchman on board, and none with a crew sufficiently large to work her. Many of these vessels never sailed again. Some rotted away and sank at their moorings. —Herbert Asbury (Chiltern Thrust Bore, 2022)

So was the fate for many, many ships that had sailed to San Francisco.

In the 1850s, America was ripe with Gold Fever. People traveled to California in droves, hoping to be the first to strike it rich. Some of these gold seekers arrived via ship—and many of those ships never left San Francisco after the gold rush had subsided.

Some of these ships found new lives as buildings—from offices, hotels, stores, and even a jail; these ships quickly became just another part of the city.

As the city of San Francisco grew up around them, these ships were eventually buried or built over. One could say that the city was literally built on these ships—with over

75 of them lying beneath the ground. There might even be more that are, currently, unaccounted for.

Chapter 61:

To Steal the President

Abraham Lincoln has gone down in history as one of the most beloved and most important presidents in the history of the United States of America. Ask any American and they could tell you about Lincoln—about how he was born in a log cabin, about how he was very tall, about his assassination… but how many people could you find that would tell you the tale of how, after he died, his corpse was almost stolen?

After President Lincoln was assassinated, his body was returned to his home in Illinois. There, his body was placed in a tomb, where he rested in peace for eleven years (Martin, 2021). Then, in 1876, thieves attempted to steal the President's corpse.

On November 7th, multiple people were startled away from the President's tomb after they attempted to break into it. They had been spotted, and a guard fired one shot into the air as a warning. All of the thieves scattered.

Eleven days later, the thieves were named—or, at least, two of them were. The Chicago Daily News published the following article.

"Jack Hughes and Torrence Mullen, two notorious characters, were arrested last night for attempted robbery, on the night of the 7th inst., of the tomb of Abraham Lincoln," the paper read. "Hughes is under indictment for counterfeiting in connection with the notorious Boyd and was out on bail" (Martin, 2021).

Though there was very little else written in the paper, historians do know a little bit more about the attempted kidnapping of the President's body. Benjamin Boyd as a counterfeiter working for the crime boss James Kennally. The Chicago police had arrested Boyd, thus stopping his work as a counterfeiter. This upset Kennally, who was probably making a lot of money off of Boyd's counterfeits.

Apparently, Hughes and Mullen both worked for the crime boss as well. When Boyd was arrested, Kennally told Hughes and Mullen to steal Abraham Lincoln's body so that they could hold it for ransom—they would return the body once Boyd was freed, and once the police handed over a large sum of money.

Of course, considering Hughes and Mullen had never grave robbed before, the plan went south, thus leading to the President's body being safe and the would-be kidnappers being arrested.

Worried that someone else would attempt to steal the President's body, Lincoln was moved to an unmarked grave within the tomb, and then later into a steel cage to keep his remains safe and sound.

No one else has since attempted to remove the remains of the beloved President, but one cannot be too careful, after all. There is a lot of history in those bones.

Conclusion

The world—and beyond—is filled with stories and mysteries that will forever capture the imaginations of humanity. While many of these stories and mysteries will never have an explanation, others will, one day, be solved.

Now that you have finished this book, I implore you to look for more strange mysteries in this world. Tell your friends and family about the amazing, unbelievable facts you have learned. Spreading knowledge about these things might lead to those that are still a mystery to become solved stories.

From how Scarface got his famous scar and nickname to why the Rainbow River in Colombia is so colorful, from the history of the Meteor Crater to the Wow! Signal's ongoing mystery, there are so many wonderful, weird, and wacky things to learn about.

From Reggae Kings to Voodoo Queens, from ships buried beneath San Francisco to Volkswagen cars rotting away in the desert, we have looked at and explored a number of interesting stories and facts. Yet there is so much more for you to discover!

The stories covered in this book are but the tip of the iceberg. There are so many more interesting and head-scratching tales out there to learn about and enjoy. That, my friend, is the wonderful thing about humanity—we are always curious and thirsty for knowledge.

Truly, this Earth—and beyond—is a wonderful, weird place. Remember to always learn, to always question, and always explore. Who knows—maybe, one day, you will be a part of a weird or unsolved fact yourself. Or, maybe, you will be the one to finally solve a decades-old mystery.

As they say, the future is in your hands.

MORE BOOKS BY HENRY BENNETT...

I hope you enjoyed this book and learned something new. Please check out some of my other publications:

EXPLORING FACTS

EXTRAORDINARY STORIES & WEIRD FACTS FROM HISTORY TRIVIA BOOK

HENRY BENNETT

Dive into...

THE
UNBELIEVABLE
FACTS
BOOK

Hilariously Weird Facts & Fascinating
Stories from Planet Earth

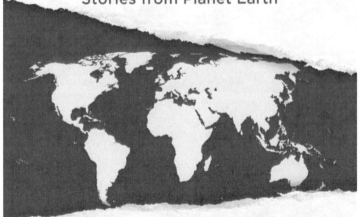

HENRY BENNETT

DON'T FORGET YOUR BONUS BOOKS!

To help you along your investing in knowledge journey, we've provided a free and exclusive copy of the short book, *Amazing Quick-Fire Facts,* and a bonus copy of book, *The Big Book of Fun Riddles & Jokes.*

We highly recommend you sign up now to get the most out of these books. You can do that by visiting https://www.subscribepage.com/henrybennett to receive your FREE copies!

References

American Museum of Natural History. (2022). American Museum of Natural History. American Museum of Natural History. https://www.amnh.org/exhibitions/permanent/meteorites/meteorite-impacts/meteor-crater

AMNH. (2015, May 4). *The Immortal Jellyfish | AMNH*. American Museum of Natural History. https://www.amnh.org/explore/news-blogs/on-exhibit-posts/the-immortal-jellyfish

Banerji, U. (2016, April 6). *The Chinese Female Pirate Who Commanded 80,000 Outlaws*. Atlas Obscura. https://www.atlasobscura.com/articles/ching-shih-chinese-female-pirate

Bate, A. (2021, July 23). *Timbuktu. History Hit*. https://www.historyhit.com/locations/timbuktu/

BBC. (2019, June 12). *History of Nintendo: Where did Nintendo come from?* - CBBC Newsround. Bbc.co.uk. https://www.bbc.co.uk/newsround/48606526

Blackwood, E. (2021, January 7). *The Dark History Behind The "London Bridge Is Falling Down" Nursery Rhyme*. All That's Interesting.

https://allthatsinteresting.com/london-bridge-is-falling-down

BLAKEMORE, E. (2022, June 14). *Why it took 50 years to resolve Canada and Denmark's dispute over a tiny Arctic island*. History. https://www.nationalgeographic.com/history/article/how-hans-island-sparked-whisky-war-between-canada-denmark

bob.hind1. (2019, May 9). *Did Buster Crabb mystery involve Lord Mountbatten?* – Retro. Www.portsmouth.co.uk. https://www.portsmouth.co.uk/retro/did-buster-crabb-mystery-involve-lord-mountbatten-retro-1315758

Braudy, L. (2018, March 1). *The history of the Hollywood sign, from public nuisance to symbol of stardom* | Britannica. Www.britannica.com. https://www.britannica.com/story/the-history-of-the-hollywood-sign

Brent, H. (2021, August 18). *Exploring Irish Mythology: The Banshee*. The Irish Post. https://www.irishpost.com/life-style/exploring-irish-mythology-banshee-170287

Captain Cook's Cruises. (2019, March 20). *Fiji Cruise Blog | What Is Firewalking in Fiji?*

Www.captaincookcruisesfiji.com.

https://www.captaincookcruisesfiji.com/blog/what-is-firewalking-in-fiji#:~:text=This%20is%20where%20the%20men

Carrabelle City Hall Office Complex. (2022). *World's Smallest Police Station*. Www.mycarrabelle.com. https://www.mycarrabelle.com/visitors/worlds-smallest-police-station/#:~:text=We%20still%20have%20our%20%E2%80%9CSmallest

Chiltern Thrust Bore. (2022). *7 of the Strangest Underground Discoveries Ever Made*. Www.chilternthrustbore.co.uk. https://www.chilternthrustbore.co.uk/blog/2015/5/7-of-the-strangest-underground-discoveries-ever-made/

CNN. (2016, December 5). *The fabulous coffins of Ghana*. CNN. https://edition.cnn.com/2016/10/14/africa/gallery/ghana-coffins-mpa/index.html

Countryfile Magazine. (2022). *Guide to Robin Hood: history of the legend and best places to visit*. Countryfile.com. https://www.countryfile.com/people/historical-figures/guide-to-robin-hood-history-of-the-legend-and-best-places-to-visit/

Crime Feed Staff. (2022, August 15). *Who Killed Biggie & Tupac? The Question Remains Over 25 Years Later*. Investigation Discovery. https://www.investigationdiscovery.com/crimefeed/murder/who-killed-biggie-tupac-the-question-remains-over-25-years-later

Cunha, B. A. (2004). *The death of Alexander the Great: malaria or typhoid fever?* Infectious Disease Clinics of North America, 18(1), 53–63. https://doi.org/10.1016/S0891-5520(03)00090-4

David, L. (2022, August 28). *Meteor crater: The hole from space that keeps on giving*. Space.com. https://www.space.com/meteor-crater-hole-from-space-lunar-surface

Davidson, L. (2021, October 11). 10 Facts About Che Guevara. History Hit. https://www.historyhit.com/facts-about-che-guevara/

Dimuro, G. (2018, March 28). *The Real Story Of Marie Laveau, New Orleans' Witchy Voodoo Queen*. All That's Interesting; All That's Interesting. https://allthatsinteresting.com/marie-laveau

Dyslexia the Gift. (2016, March 8). *Leonardo da Vinci | Dyslexia the Gift*. Www.dyslexia.com. https://www.dyslexia.com/famous/leonardo-da-vinci/

Ewing, H. (1927). *Santa Claus receives aeroplane pilot's license from Assistant Secretary of Commerce. Although there may not be sufficient snow for his reindeer sleigh, Santa Claus will still be able to deliver his load of presents on time this Christmas by using the air route. The old saint called at the Commerce Department in Washington today where he is shown receiving an aeroplane pilot's license from Assistant Secretary of Commerce. for Aeronautics William P. MacCracken, while Clarence M. Young (right) Director of Aeronautics, Department of Commerce, looks on. Airway maps and the assurance that the lights would be burning on the airways Christmas Eve were also given to Santa.* Www.loc.gov. https://www.loc.gov/pictures/item/2016888549/

Ewing, J. (2019, May 6). *Six Years Ago, He Helped Expose VW's Diesel Fraud. This Year, G.M. Let Him Go.* (Published 2019). The New York Times. https://www.nytimes.com/2019/05/06/business/her manth-kappanna-vw-emissions-gm.html

Gabe Paoletti. (2017, December 6). *Meet Hiroo Onoda, The Soldier Who Kept Fighting World War II For 29 Years After It Ended.* All That's Interesting; All That's Interesting. https://allthatsinteresting.com/hiroo-onoda

Gladden, D. (2021, October 26). *Mysterious History – The Fouke Monster*. SWARK Today. https://swark.today/mysterious-history-the-fouke-monster/

Greer, J. (2022, February 13). *Who is Snoop Dogg? Age, net worth, real name & more to know about Super Bowl halftime performer*. Www.sportingnews.com. https://www.sportingnews.com/us/nfl/news/snoop-dogg-age-net-worth-real-name-super-bowl/sya3amiaqja8rbop01exeboj#:~:text=What%20is%20Snoop%20Dogg

Hanton, A. (2020, October 23). *A Brief History Of South Korea's Weirdest Urban Legend: Killer Fans*. Cracked.com. https://www.cracked.com/article_28829_a-brief-history-south-koreas-weirdest-urban-legend-killer-fans.html

Hayes, A. (2019). *Satoshi Nakamoto*. Investopedia. https://www.investopedia.com/terms/s/satoshi-nakamoto.asp

Hayes, A. (2022, August 20). *Tulip Mania: About the Dutch Tulip Bulb Market Bubble*. Investopedia. https://www.investopedia.com/terms/d/dutch_tulip_

bulb_market_bubble.asp#:~:text=It%20occurred%20i
n%20Holland%20during

History Channel Editors. (2010, May 5). *The Real Robin Hood*. HISTORY.
https://www.history.com/topics/british-history/robin-hood#:~:text=While%20most%20contemporary%20sc
holars%20have

Hodsdon, E. (2021, February 5). *Darius the Great: 9 Facts About The King Of Kings*. TheCollector.
https://www.thecollector.com/darius-the-great-king-of-kings/

Homer, A. (2020). *What Is the Oak Island Money Pit?* HISTORY. https://www.history.com/shows/the-curse-of-oak-island/articles/what-is-the-money-pit

Homiak, J. (2021, February 26). *Black History in Roots Reggae Music*. Smithsonian Center for Folklife and Cultural Heritage.
https://folklife.si.edu/magazine/black-history-in-roots-reggae-music#:~:text=Since%20the%20late%201960s%2C%2
0reggae

Hughes, B. (2021, October 23). *10 Interesting Facts About Al Capone*. HistoryColored.
https://historycolored.com/articles/8129/10-interesting-facts-about-al-capone/

Humphrys, J. (2022). *What pet did Lord Byron keep at Cambridge University?* Historyrevealed.com. https://www.historyrevealed.com/eras/victorians/what-pet-did-lord-byron-keep-at-cambridge-university/

Hunt, K. (2022). *Swedish Blood Donors Get A Text Message When Their Blood Saves A Life*. Everplans. https://www.everplans.com/articles/swedish-blood-donors-get-a-text-message-when-their-blood-saves-a-life#:~:text=As%20the%20tweets%20and%20Instagrams

Italy Magazine. (2007, September 7). *Mona Lisa self-portrait*. Italy Magazine. https://www.italymagazine.com/featured-story/mona-lisa-self-portrait#:~:text=The%20Mona%20Lisa%20is%20a

Jacobs, D. (2019, July 19). *The Volkswagen Diesel Emissions Scandal and Accountability* - The CPA Journal. The CPA Journal. https://www.cpajournal.com/2019/07/22/9187/

Jarus, O. (2016, August 16). *10 Biggest Historical Mysteries That Will Probably Never Be Solved*. Live Science; Live Science. https://www.livescience.com/11361-history-overlooked-mysteries.html

Jensen, K. T. (2017, June 23). *Crocodile Dundee Was Based On A Real Aussie.* OMGFacts. http://omgfacts.com/crocodile-dundee-was-based-on-a-real-aussie/

Jha, A. (2007, April 13). *Who are you calling chicken? T. rex's closest living relative found on the farm.* The Guardian. https://www.theguardian.com/science/2007/apr/13/uknews.taxonomy

Johnson, B. B., & Russell, D. (2022, June 24). *Krakatau: The loudest sound in recorded history.* Www.wbur.org. https://www.wbur.org/endlessthread/2022/06/24/krakatau-loudest-sound

k2forma. (2018, March 29). *Best Plants that Naturally Repel Snakes | Updated for 2021.* Pests.org. https://www.pests.org/best-plants-that-naturally-repel-snakes/

Kiger, P. J. (2015, February 20). 9 *"Unsolved" Mysteries That Have Been Solved.* HowStuffWorks. https://science.howstuffworks.com/science-vs-myth/unexplained-phenomena/10-unsolved-mysteries-that-have-been-solved.htm

Knauer, K. (2017, April 6). *I Want You: The Story Behind the Iconic Recruitment Poster*. Time; Time. https://time.com/4725856/uncle-sam-poster-history/

Korpar, L. (2021, December 31). *"Raining fish" explained: Storm brings in fish falling from sky in rare Texas phenomenon*. Newsweek. https://www.newsweek.com/raining-fish-explained-storm-brings-fish-falling-sky-texas-1664747

KRULWICH, R. (2010, May 28). *Aliens Found In Ohio? The "Wow!" Signal*. NPR.org. https://www.npr.org/sections/krulwich/2010/05/28/126510251/aliens-found-in-ohio-the-wow-signal

LaGrave, K. (2017, June 17). *Japan Has a Desert, and It's Awesome*. Condé Nast Traveler. https://www.cntraveler.com/story/japans-tottori-sand-dunes-look-straight-out-of-the-sahara-desert

Londonist. (2013, April 18). *London Bridge Sold To An American, 45 Years Ago Today*. Londonist. https://londonist.com/2013/04/londonbridge

Loxton, A. (2019, October 31). *10 Facts About Guy Fawkes: Britain's Most Infamous Villain*? History Hit. https://www.historyhit.com/thrilling-facts-about-guy-fawkes/

Martin, A. (2021, April 15). *This week in history: Plot to steal Abraham Lincoln's body foiled.* Chicago Sun-Times. https://chicago.suntimes.com/2021/4/15/22382530/abraham-lincolns-body-stolen-plot#:~:text=On%20Nov.

McConnaughhay, A. (2022, May 13). *The Rainbow River of Colombia - Caño Cristales in La Macarena, Colombia* - Cartagena Explorer. Cartagena Explorer. https://www.cartagenaexplorer.com/rainbow-river-colombia-cano-cristales/

McFadden, R. D. (2014, January 17). *Hiroo Onoda, Soldier Who Hid in Jungle for Decades, Dies at 91.* The New York Times. https://www.nytimes.com/2014/01/18/world/asia/hiroo-onoda-imperial-japanese-army-officer-dies-at-91.html

Milmo, D. (2022, August 6). *Another court case fails to unlock the mystery of bitcoin's Satoshi Nakamoto.* The Guardian. https://www.theguardian.com/technology/2022/aug/06/another-court-case-fails-to-unlock-the-mystery-of-bitcoins-satoshi-nakamoto

Monstro Productions. (2011). *Fouke Monster: The Legend of Boggy Creek*. Www.foukemonster.net. http://www.foukemonster.net/

Nelson, B. (2019, March 1). *10 of the World's Biggest Unsolved Mysteries. Treehugger.* https://www.treehugger.com/worlds-biggest-unsolved-mysteries-4869324

Ockham's Notebook. (2019, December 27). *Genghis Khan Was a Progressive Humanitarian Who Sparked the Western Enlightenment*. Ockham's Notebook. https://ockhamsnotebook.com/2019/12/27/genghis-khan-was-a-progressive-humanitarian-who-sparked-the-western-enlightenment/#:~:text=He%20was%20ahead%20of%20his

Papadopoulos, L. (2022, July 29). *All about the only car to break the sound barrier: the Thrust SSC*. Interestingengineering.com. https://interestingengineering.com/innovation/all-about-the-only-car-to-break-the-sound-barrier-the-thrust-ssc

PATOWARY, K. (2016, September 6). *The Mysterious Toynbee Tiles*. Www.amusingplanet.com. https://www.amusingplanet.com/2016/09/the-mysterious-toynbee-tiles.html

Raga, S. (2016, November 22). *Who Was the Mysterious Babushka Lady at JFK's Assassination?* Mentalfloss.com. https://www.mentalfloss.com/article/72245/who-was-mysterious-babushka-lady-jfks-assassination

Richter, D. (2013, January 25). *The Fall of Siam & the Lost Temples of Ayutthaya*. Ex Utopia. https://www.exutopia.com/dark-tourism-temples-of-ayutthaya-thailand/

SAINSBURY, B. (2021, December 14). *The Frogman Who Vanished: What Happened to the Royal Navy's Most Celebrated Diver, Lionel "Buster" Crabb?* HistoryNet. https://www.historynet.com/the-frogman-who-vanished-what-happened-to-the-royal-navys-most-celebrated-diver-lionel-buster-crabb/

Salem Media. (2017, May 11). *Mongol Empire and Religious Freedom* - History. History. https://www.historyonthenet.com/mongol-empire-and-religious-freedom

Schwartz, L. (2018, August 20). *Here Are The 13 Artworks Stolen The Night Of The Gardner Museum Heist*. Www.wbur.org. https://www.wbur.org/news/2018/08/20/lastseen-gardner-heist-missing-art

Serena, K. (2017, September 27). *How Jack The Baboon Worked On A Railway For 9 Years Without Ever Messing Up*. All That's Interesting. https://allthatsinteresting.com/jack-the-baboon

SHAPIRO, A. (2015, August 5). *South Korea's Quirky Notions About Electric Fans*. NPR.org. https://www.npr.org/sections/parallels/2015/08/09/430341089/south-koreas-quirky-notions-about-electric-fans

Smee, T. (2018, August 24). *"Limeys" - The Story Behind the Slang Term Given to the British*. Thevintagenews. https://www.thevintagenews.com/2018/08/24/limey/?chrome=1

Smithfield, B. (2016, July 14). *In 1907 swimmer Annette Kellermann was arrested for wearing one piece swimsuit , afterwards, she marketed her own line & revolutionized womens swimwear*. Thevintagenews. https://www.thevintagenews.com/2016/07/14/in-1907-swimmer-annette-kellermann-was-arrested-for-wearing-one-piece-swimsuit-afterwards-she-marketed-her-own-line-revolutionized-womens-swimwear/?chrome=1

Specktor, B. (2022, June 25). *Bizarre "polygons" are cracking through the surface of Mars.* Livescience.com. https://www.livescience.com/mars-polygons-ice-sublimation

spoonbillhank. (2019, November 18). *The Day It Rained Eels.* The Fisheries Blog. https://thefisheriesblog.com/2019/11/18/the-day-it-rained-eels/

Stilwell, B. (2022, February 2). *Love the McDonald's drive-thru? Thank the military.* We Are the Mighty. https://www.wearethemighty.com/popular/can-thank-military-mcdonalds-drive-thru/

Super Simple. (2019, March 20). *The history of the ship in a bottle.* Super Simple. https://supersimple.com/article/the-history-of-the-ship-in-a-bottle/

TAYLOR, D. (2020, December 2). *Morning Start: Santa Claus has an official pilot's license.* Salmon Arm Observer. https://www.saobserver.net/trending-now/morning-start-santa-claus-has-an-official-pilots-license/

The Editors of Encyclopaedia Britannica. (2022). *Althing* | History & Facts. Encyclopedia Britannica. https://www.britannica.com/topic/Althing

The Editors of the Encyclopaedia Britannica. (2019). *Yi Sun-shin | Korean admiral.* In Encyclopædia Britannica. https://www.britannica.com/biography/Yi-Sun-shin

The Parliament House. (n.d.). *The Parliament House. Alþingi.* Retrieved September 17, 2022, from https://www.althingi.is/english/about-the-parliament/the-parliament-house/

UK Parliament. (2013). *State Opening: Elements unseen by the public.* UK Parliament. https://www.parliament.uk/about/living-heritage/evolutionofparliament/parliamentwork/offices-and-ceremonies/overview/state-opening/elements-unseen-by-the-public/

Walbank, F. W. (2018). *Alexander the Great | Biography, Empire, & Facts.* In Encyclopædia Britannica. https://www.britannica.com/biography/Alexander-the-Great

Wamsley, L. (2018, March 29). *Why 300,000 Volkswagens Are Being Stored In These Massive Auto Boneyards.* NPR. https://www.npr.org/sections/thetwo-way/2018/03/29/597991227/why-300-000-

volkswagens-are-being-stored-in-these-massive-auto-boneyards

Whittington, M. R. (2022, August 14). *NASA might cancel mission to massive "gold mine asteroid" — here's why it shouldn't*. The Hill. https://thehill.com/opinion/technology/3597381-nasa-might-cancel-mission-to-massive-gold-mine-asteroid-heres-why-it-shouldnt/#:~:text=Until%20recently%2C%20scientists%20thought%20that

Wikipedia. (2022, February 1). *Fan death*. Wikipedia. https://en.wikipedia.org/wiki/Fan_death

WorldAtlas. (2018, August 21). *10 Interesting Facts About Fiji*. WorldAtlas. https://www.worldatlas.com/articles/10-interesting-facts-about-fiji.html

Made in United States
North Haven, CT
20 November 2022

26974683R00117